Why People Enjoy this Book...

"It was such a joy to open up this book and read such beautiful suggestions for raising Catholic children."

— *Marcella Goeckner, Mother, Cottonwood, ID*

"GUIDING has made a great hit with my Pastor . . . (I will give) each new family a book at the baptism of their first child."

— *Catherine Kleinweber, Mother, Nebraska City, NE*

"This is the kind of book customers will get more copies to give as gifts to their brothers, sisters and friends. It's all so down to earth and full of good ideas for their kids. I would suggest it to all parents who come in the store."

— *Barb Gaskell, Owner, St. Raphael Bookstore, Canton, OH*

"Your book is just what our young moms are looking for! . . . And your book will be a God-send for so many moms."

— *Sister Alice Ruane, Director of Religious Education*
Saint Daniel the Prophet Catholic Church, Scottsdale, AZ

"I shared some ideas from your book at our first meeting. The response was overwhelming!"

— *Annette Manze, Mom's Support Group Leader, Gainesville, FL*

"Two of my grandchildren are coming next Friday . . . I thought perhaps I could use your book while they are here."

— *Catherine O'Hara, Grandmother, Estes Park, CO*

"I think it's well done and I would like to distribute one to all my parishioners who have preschoolers."

— *Fr. George Sivoes, O.M.I., Pastor*
Saint Mary of Lourdes, Lincoln ME

Published by
GOOD CATHOLIC BOOKS
Box 26144, Cleveland, OH 44126

ISBN: 0-9638235-0-7
Library of Congress Catalog Card Number: 96-770207

SIXTH PRINTING
June 1996

Cover Design and Layout by
RON WIGGINS
Typeset by
JOE VANTAGGI

Printed in the United States of America

Dedication

To Our Lady,
The Blessed Mother of us all,
without whom this book would never have been written

GUIDING YOUR
Catholic Preschooler

"Train a child in the way he should go;
Even when he is old,
He will not swerve from it."
— *Proverbs 22:6*

Kathy Pierce
with
Lori Rowland

Acknowledgments

My first thanks go to my Mom and Dad, Ken and Leitner Greiner. WOW! How do you thank your parents? First, they taught me the Catholic faith...so few words for so much meaning! They opened the gates of eternal life to me and my family. More recently, if it weren't for them, this book would still be in a rough draft! For the hours of reading, editing, typing, daughter-prodding, prayerful and financial support, baby-sitting while I worked...Thank You.

Thank you Larry, my husband, for being my best friend...It must have been difficult living with a pregnant lady who was writing a book. And to my children, for the opportunity to share the Catholic faith. They're so eager to learn, so anxious about God...if we could only imitate their enthusiasm!

A special thank you to Lori and Paul Rowland, some of my very best friends in Christ. There are several chapters to their credit as well as countless hours of editing and proofing. For it was Lori who helped me realize that I was not alone in trying to not only teach but help my children LIVE their faith. She promised me that I wasn't "too overprotective, too religious or fanatical" and all the other adjectives I've been called.

Many thanks to Jeanne (Kirby) Gorman, Mary Jo Ogle, and Linda Bauman for their tireless help; Wanda Mead and Warpha Lunnon in Phoenix for their help.

A big thank you to the GOOD CATHOLIC BOOKS team of Katie Hofman, Margot Davidson, Tom Baugh, Steve and Kathy DiCarlo, Bill Whitmore and his lovely wife Therese for the new and improved edition. Their excitement, energetic enthusiasm and love for children and the Church have been the key ingredients to its success. A special thanks to Bud Macfarlane, Jr, The Mary Foundation and Saint Jude Media.

Although she probably would not like the attention, I would like to thank Saint Therese of the Child Jesus, the Little Flower. It's her expression of the "little ways" that have helped me realize the importance of my vocation.

Finally and most importantly, a glorious, honorable, well-deserved, best-thanks ever to Mother Mary for being there for me from the beginning, and continuing my journey with me everyday. She has enveloped me in her mantle often. Without her guidance, help, support, prayers and love I would be more distant from her Son. In desperately fleeing, to her Immaculate Heart. I hope to come to the presence of His Most Sacred Heart. I hope that through it's fruits my work can be pleasing to her and her Son. I want more than anything for my children and all people to be with her one day.

Foreword

November 1992

In an age of alluring toys and beeping technology, it is encouraging to see young parents experiencing the joy of parenthood, and passing on the spiritual truths and practices of the Catholic faith to their family in the early formative years.

Kathy Pierce, a mother of four children under the age of eight, and her husband Larry, are loving parents. She is an involved and active member of Epiphany Parish. Among other things, she has taught Vacation Bible School and religious classes for the Pre-K toddlers.

Lori Rowland and her husband, Paul, are raising three children under the age of seven. They were active in St. Charles Parish, and have recently moved to Jacksonville, Florida.

Kathy found Catholic material for older children, but very little for small folk. The practical day to day suggestions for Catholic child faith development came from combined ideas and practices that she and Lori have put down in this book - hoping that since it worked for them, others might find it helpful.

To teach one to see beyond the external comes from a persistent spiritual frame of reference. It builds on inherited tendencies and redirects behavioral patterns. Kathy makes spiritual things fun and has "simplified" the mysteries of the Catholic Faith in a way that toddlers can assimilate at their level, and love doing it. I think this book offers hundreds of helps, but basically confirms that children are intrinsically religious if only the opportunities are offered. At an early age they can appreciate sacred space (the house of God), time (seasons), and people (saints). Her frequent ear-whispering at daily Mass must make attentiveness at Sunday Mass easier. The ground rules have already been set.

I heartily congratulate Kathy for sharing her experiences and efforts with us at Epiphany and with all her readers.

Rev. John Michalicka, Pastor
Epiphany of the Lord Catholic Church
Oklahoma City, OK

Contents

Chapter 1

Like arrows in the hand of the warrior are the
children of one's youth.   Happy is the man who
has his quiver full of them!   (Psalm 127:4,5)

Introduction

A young child's mind is ready to absorb, process and retain
an enormous quantity of information! As parents, you watch
your child discover a vast scope of secular information about
the world around him every day! A child can begin learning
about the rich tradition and ritual of the Catholic faith as
well.

Many Catholic churches do not begin formal weekly Religious Education until a child is four or five years old. Parents teach a child a wealth of information about the world
around him and how to live in society long before the first
day of Sunday School. Parents teach every day. They should
accept responsibility to teach the Catholic Faith every day,
too.

Do not expect priests and religious education teachers to
carry the burden of teaching all there is about the Catholic
faith. Strive every day to keep the commitment you made
when you had your child baptized. Realize and appreciate
your vocation of motherhood and fatherhood. Fulfilling your
responsibility will take time and effort. God will reward you
abundantly!

Your Primary Goal

Your primary goal as the parent of a young child must be to teach him to know, love and serve the Three Persons of the Holy Trinity and to develop a loving relationship with Mary, our Blessed Mother. When he gets older and is challenged in his faith, it will be difficult and perhaps impossible for him to desert God and Mary. His strong personal relationship and his love for Them will be lasting.

Any relationship takes time and effort to develop. This is true whether it be family, a friend or God. Help your child know God, so he can love Him. You cannot love someone you do not know! The more you and your child put into this friendship, the more you both will gain from it.

Mary can become a best friend, as a true mother. She is an advocate. She can go to God asking a favor. Developing a relationship with her will bring you and your child closer to Jesus, her son and the Holy Spirit, her spouse. Her mission is to bring you to God!

Set an Example

A young child learns by example. He will imitate you. He will imitate the way you act, eat, dress and worship. Therefore, it is essential that you set a good example in your spiritual life. If religion is important to you, it will be important to him.

Let your child see and hear you happily exercise your faith in your daily life. Be sure he sees you pray, read your Bible, attend Mass, give alms, and participate in the Sacrament of Reconciliation. Talk about your faith with him. Integrate your faith with your life. Set guidelines and stick to them. For example, since you must attend Mass on Sunday, be sure you attend Mass even if you are out of town or on vacation.

Give meaning and excitement to what you do with your religion. Your values will be transmitted to your child. Always continue to grow and learn in your faith. Read books, watch educational videos, attend retreats. Make time to develop your own relationship with your Creator in the same way you want your child to grow in his relationship with you.

When to Start

Start when your child is born. If you have missed this moment, start now! There are many ideas included in this book which you can use from day one, and it's never too late to begin! Lay the foundation early for further education. He's so eager to learn when he is very young, and he trusts and believes all you teach him. Take advantage of it!

Be alert for good opportunities to teach. Do not pass a religious book or article without mentioning it to your child. Throughout your day watch for good things for which to be thankful. Integrate prayer and God into every action including meals, bedtime, discipline and the host of activities and experiences you have each day. This book will help you get started. You're sure to develop and implement many more ideas as you and your child's relationship with God grows.

Where to Start

First teach your child about God the Father, Jesus, The Holy Spirit and Mary. They are real. They know and love your child. Do not suggest to your child that "some people do not believe in God" or "some people do not think Jesus is God." Young children shouldn't doubt. They shouldn't be introduced to the dissension which has occurred in the Church. They should trust and believe what you tell them! As they get older, they will be exposed to other religions. At that time you can explain that some people have a hard time believing all the Catholic Church teaches. You can explain that often these people don't fully understand Jesus and His teachings. We must not judge these people, but we must pray for them.

Teach your child about Old and New Testament characters. Teach him these were real people with real, live faith and love of God! Protestants introduce very young children to these characters. Yet some Catholics shy away from teaching the Bible to their children. We may even tend to become judgmental of those who sometimes seem so knowledgeable. Don't be afraid or hesitant! Learn by doing and reading! Learn with your child. Pray with your child. Open yourself to grow in your relationship with God as you teach your child.

Include the saints. They're special friends of God. As you teach about them, they'll become your friends.

More Than One Child

It's important to talk to each child at his own level. What you point out and explain to your two-year-old during Mass will be much more simple and "tangible" than what you teach your four-year-old. The questions that come from each will be different too! Do not feel bad if you cannot answer a question. Make a promise to take the time to research the answer.

Pray with each child. Talk of God with each of them every day. Avoid focusing on one child, causing another to receive less attention. Finally, resist getting tired or bored with teaching religion to the last child in line. He is just as eager and willing to learn as the first!

Working Mothers/Single Parents

Although this book was written by two mothers who stay at home, both worked for several years while their children attended day care. As cooking and cleaning are difficult to fit into your schedule, so is religious education. However, teaching your faith is still essential and very possible. Make time to teach your child about God. Do not let a secular world interfere with your primary responsibility and joy as a Catholic parent!

Daddy is Important

Mothers, pray for your child's father. Pray that he understands and appreciates the importance of his role in his child's life.

Mothers, praise dad's involvement with his child, "Honey, I like the way you explained to Tommy how trains work," or "Honey, you're very good with Annie and her baby dolls," or "you are very patient with John and I appreciate it." Brag about dad. Let dad know he is valuable and appreciated. This will encourage him to increase his contact with the child.

Many daddies do not believe that their role is important to their child's development. Nothing could be further from the truth. Daddy, realize that your example is important. Participate with your child in his play, work, sports, education and prayer. The rewards will be limitless!

Daddies, become involved in your child's religious education, too. Take your child to Sunday School. Take him to Mass. Help him make the Sign of the Cross. Encourage good behavior at Church. Read Bible stories to him. Let your child see and hear you pray. Use Saint Joseph as your example. Saint Joseph was a good Jewish father. He went to the synagogue every week and celebrated all the holidays and traditions. He passed these down to Jesus. He was a good provider and teacher. He was a hard working carpenter, and he taught Jesus his trade. Saint Joseph was also a good spouse to Mary. He was protective and gentle, loving and firm. He was a prayerful man, his mind always open and obedient to the will of God.

Saint Joseph was a man of action. When he felt God leading and directing him, he acted. In the middle of the night, when asked to go to Egypt, he wasted no time in responding.

Ask Saint Joseph to guide you in your vocation as a father. Ask him to pray with you to the Father that you may imitate him in his role as Father of Jesus.

Your Friends

Choose adult friends with whom you share the same values and priorities. Encourage play time and friendships between their child and yours. Do not be afraid or ashamed to teach your child religion. Use religion as you lovingly discipline your child while you are with these friends. Jesus said that following Him would not always be easy. Situations will arise when you have to decide between your faith and peer pressure from friends. For example, what movie or video is "everyone" seeing? Do you feel it is appropriate for your child? What about telling a "white lie" that your child overhears? Do you tell a ticket seller that he is younger than he is so you can get a cheaper entry fee? Everyone else is doing it! Be prepared for these situations. Be determined when the time comes to face these issues.

If your friends become critical, non-supportive or disrespectful of you and your decisions, you must evaluate the quality and importance of your friendship. You must also evaluate why they feel the way they do and be careful not to be judgmental of them.

Always put God first, your family next and everything else follows. These are your priorities!

Your Home

You may find your home becoming filled with religious articles, books and other signs of your faith. For the sake of you and your child's spiritual growth, this is helpful. Do what is comfortable for you and your family. In your own home, practice your faith the way you feel is best. Do what is necessary for you and your family to continually grow in your faith and devotion. Do not be concerned with the opinion of your friends. Your family comes first. If your example affects your friends and their child, consider this a fringe benefit which is pleasing to God!

Spiritual growth will not come from a sign in your front yard or around your neck saying "I'm a Catholic and proud of it!" But you do want frequent visual reminders of the most important people in your life. When you see a family photograph taken long ago, it triggers memories and thoughts. This is also true of religious articles. They trigger special thoughts and prayers throughout each day.

Using This Book
This book contains several specific ideas to help you get started immediately. Many are short and simple. Some will require a little preparation on your part. Some you will probably question as to whether or not they are appropriate for your child.

Do not try to implement all of these suggestions simultaneously. Select an idea which appeals to you. Then set a goal for your child and for yourself. As you reach one goal, add another. For example, start today reading the Children's Bible once a day to your child. Next month work on the Sign of the Cross while continuing to read the Bible. Allow your child the opportunity to grow in his spiritual knowledge! Remember, every little success contributes to the child's overall vision of his faith. Any progress, no matter how small it may seem, will be better than the alternative. God will be pleased. Never will your efforts be in vain. Always your efforts will be rewarded!

Ask God to Help You
Pray for guidance. God will help you teach your child. He will guide you if you ask Him. After all, no one knows your child better than you and God!

Chapter 2

First of all. I urge that petitions, prayers, intercessions and thanksgivings be offered for all men...Prayer of this kind is good, and God our Savior is pleased with it, for he wants all men to be saved and come to the truth.
(1 Timothy 2:1,3-4)

Prayer

Teach Your Child to Pray

Praying is communicating with God and should be part of your way of life. It is not a separate activity for special occasions. Praying every day is vital for you and your child. Teaching your child to pray every day helps him develop a relationship with God. It is your most important responsibility as a parent.

Set a good example of a prayerful life. Set aside quiet time for your own personal prayers. Your child can join you, but these are your prayers. There is no better teacher than good example by a parent. Do not allow prayer to become monotonous and boring. If your child is restless, change your pattern of prayer. You do not want prayer to become a dreaded chore.

Begin when the child is in the womb. He hears and feels your thoughts and prayers before birth. Continue when your child is born, still an infant. The more you pray with him, formally and informally, the more spontaneous and natural prayer will be in his life.

Over the years, the important relationship with God the Father, the Son and the Holy Spirit will be formed and developed through prayer. A stable, strong foundation will be built. As the child grows, he may challenge this friendship with God experiencing good times and bad. However, the stronger the foundation and the more time and effort given in prayer to developing an intensive love and incredible faith, then the more the friendship will be affirmed. God will be there for your child. Encourage him always to turn to God every day, and he'll learn to do it on his own! Prayer will become his way of life.

When to Pray

Pray in the morning and in the evening. Pray at nap time and play time. Pray on a walk, driving in the car, when you hear a siren and when you eat a meal. Pray when something special or good happens to you or your family, or in time of sorrow. Pray in time of need. Say prayers of thanksgiving. Pray formally and informally. Pray any time you think of it. Pray often.

Pray as a Family

Include your entire family together in prayer daily. This can be meal time, bed time, or after dinner before television or toys.

Mention why you're praying: "It makes God happy when we talk to Him. He is so good to us and is so special. It's important we talk with Him every day! Let's see, what special things shall we pray for today?" This can lead to a moment of silence before prayer. This quiet time will open your hearts to God and will help create a special relationship with Him that cannot be achieved any other way. Prayer's a rich family tradition and will certainly change and grow as your child gets older. For example, you could grow into praying a rosary together on a regular schedule.

Learning the Sign of the Cross
The sign of the cross is how we say "Hello" and "Good-bye" to God when we talk to Him in formal prayer. We're inviting Him to be with us. We honor and glorify the name of God with the sign of the cross. We're also shielding ourselves against evil.

Children love to color, outline and trace. When we make the sign of the cross, we are "tracing" God's love for us. We're asking the three persons of the Trinity to envelope us! It's important your child learn this early. He'll learn to do this by watching and imitating you.

A helpful trick in teaching the sign of the cross is to use your left hand instead of the right, and touch your right shoulder first instead of the correct left. Your child will copy. He'll stare at you and imitate your hand movement. He'll look like your mirror image!

As an alternative, have the child sit beside you while looking in the mirror. Have him copy your movements. He'll then be doing it correctly.

Allowing your child to make these movements on his own will make a stronger impression than your holding his right hand, guiding his movements and then having him repeat from memory. Slowly say the words, "In the name of the Father and of the Son and of the Holy Spirit. Amen," as you cross yourself. Over time your child will begin to repeat you, then finally say it with you!

Don't be strict and impatient if he makes a mistake. You don't want to frustrate him. Instead, praise his efforts. He's trying! He's proud of himself! He's learning!

Morning Prayer
You should pray every morning before you ever see your child. The Lord's Prayer is appropriate as is a simple plea, "Lord,

help me do Your Will today." "Mother Mary, be my guide today. Help me lead my kids to your Son."

Keep a candle on your kitchen table. Light the candle, say your prayer, then allow the child to blow out the candle! In fact, if you have more than one child, you may have to re-light it for each child to blow out (or collect more candles)! Perhaps a meal time habit will be formed.

The candle is important because it helps keep the child's attention. Also, you can tell the child that Jesus is like the light of the candle. He's the Light of the world! He's bright and makes people feel happy.

He must complete his prayers before he blows out the candle:

1. Make the sign of the cross ("Hello, God")
2. Hold his hands in prayer.
3. Say the same prayer every day. Repetition is important to assist in memorizing the prayer. A good prayer is this: "Oh Jesus, I give you today, all that I think and do and say. Amen"

   After he learns this prayer you can expand it: "Dear Mary and God, please help me today with all that I think and do and say. Amen." Another good prayer is to your guardian angel which can be found in the LEARNING ABOUT ANGELS section of this book. A two-year old can memorize these prayers.
4. Make the sign of the cross again. ("Good Bye, God")

5. <u>Then</u> he can blow out the candle!

If you forget to pray at breakfast, say a prayer any time that you remember. Driving in the car or dressing your child are good times to offer the day to God!

Praying the Rosary

The rosary is a gift from Mary. It's a tool for us to contemplate the New Testament, specifically the mysteries of Our Lord. Mary asks us to pray the rosary. She wants us to become closer to her Son by meditating on His life, death, resurrection and glorification. It can become one of the most meaningful avenues for contemplative prayer, the most intimate form of prayer. With the exception of the Holy Eucharist and Sacred Scripture, it is the deepest form of communion we have with God. Your relationship with the Blessed Mother and Her Son will only blossom as your devotion and commitment to the holy rosary grows. Do not deprive your child of developing such an awesome, inspiring and incomprehensibly beautiful relationship with God and Our Lady.

"I Don't Know the Rosary; How can I Set an Example?"

Learn by doing! There are countless books and holy cards available which will guide you through the actual prayers and Mysteries of the Rosary. Many will teach you the Fruits of the Mysteries as well. Have one of these books or cards with you as you say the prayers. The rosary may seem monotonous. You may feel your mind wander. Do not give up! Bring your heart back to your prayers. (See the back pages of this book for: HOW TO PRAY THE ROSARY)

When you have accomplished this, you can pray the rosary any time throughout your day without a lot of concentration on "what comes next." At times you may need to listen to God. This could become contemplative prayer, a time when Our Lord and Our Lady will speak to you in a quiet way. Open your heart and let Them in!

Your Child and the Rosary

Allow your child frequent access to a rosary. Let him see your rosary next to your bed, in your purse or pocket, or perhaps in the car. Keep one near his bed and within his reach. Let him touch it and hold it. Let him know it is special. No throwing, swinging or hitting with it. If that happens, you will take it away! Be even more protective if the rosary has been blessed!

Buy him his own rosary. This can be very inexpensive and safe. For young children, one to three years old, find one of string and plastic beads or of knotted cord. Avoid the small chain link rosaries. These can break, be swallowed or scratch sensitive skin. As your child gets older he can be given more responsibility to carefully care for his own rosary.

Arrange for your child to hear the rosary being said on a regular basis. This can be done in several ways:

1. Say it yourself, in a low whisper, in the child's room, after you have said his nightly prayers with him. He can hold his own rosary while he listens to you and as he falls asleep. He will fall asleep in prayer!

2. Go to Mass 15-20 minutes early with your child. Say the rosary together before the Blessed Sacrament. Your child will play on the seat and climb over your legs, but he is hearing and subconsciously absorbing the prayers!

3. Pray the rosary as a family at home. Turn off the television, go to your room, unplug the phone, kneel and take a few minutes to pray together. Your child can hold his own rosary and "pray" with it while the older family members pray. As your child grows up, he will look back on these special family prayerful times with fond memories.

4. Say the rosary on car trips, even short trips. Let him hear it being said while traveling.

5. Say only a decade of the rosary with him on occasion, especially if time does not allow the entire rosary. This is brief, but nice.

6. Find a book with pictures depicting each mystery. Allow your child to hold and display to your family the picture of the mystery you are contemplating.

7. As your children get older, allow them to lead decades of the rosary. They will take great pride in active participation.

Bedtime Prayers

Always, always end the day in prayer. You should pray if the child only listens, or even if he is not listening! Never force him to repeat after you. Expect his participation to be better some nights than others! He may sit on his knees very reverently with his hands folded and repeat after you word for word, or he may lay down and fall asleep in the middle of the Lord's Prayer. He's little, and he learns by example. if you force him to repeat prayers, it could lead to resentment and negative feelings about prayer. Continue to close every day with prayer!

After making the sign of the cross, pray the Lord's Prayer, the Hail Mary and the Glory Be. if your child is really very tired, say only these prayers, but always say these three. If he is not so tired, add spontaneous prayers.

Pray as many spontaneous prayers as you would like. Ask for blessings for immediate family and for friends. You can add prayers of thanksgiving for things you did or gifts received from God throughout the day. You can thank God for the rain or sun, for "my bed," or for that great lunch his friend's mom made for him!

You can add "help me learn" prayers relating to situations your child encountered that day: "Help me learn to share my toys, to be nice to my friends, not to hit my brother any more, to mind mom and dad." "I'm sorry for jumping on the furniture" or "pushing/hitting my friend. I will really try and do better."

Add "take care" prayers and begin helping him realize how fortunate and blessed he is. "Take care of kids who don't have mommies or daddies. Take care of people who are cold tonight because they don't have a house to keep them warm, and for people who are hungry." This may seem like a strange thing to pray for with a young child. He may not really understand what you are saying. As he gets a little older, he will ask about these people. It will allow you to teach him almsgiving, and giving of clothes and food to the poor. Limit your prayers for social issues! You do not want to worry, depress or scare your child! Keep it as light as possible. As he gets older, pray for resolutions of specific situations which occur in his life or in the world. (Be careful not to do this when he is very young.)

As your child gets older, bedtime is a good time to memorize new prayers such as the Act of Contrition, Hail Holy Queen, and Prayer to the Holy Spirit.

End your prayers by saying, "I love You God. I love You, Jesus. I love You, Mary. Amen." This is simple and your child will soon be able to say it with you. It is a definitive ending. He knows you are finished praying. Finally, it is a good, positive, happy prayer in and of itself!

Close by making the sign of the cross.

When you kiss your child good-night say, "I love you and God loves you too because you are so special. And you love God, too! He made you a special kid, you know." Say this to him frequently.

Also, bless your child as you close your prayers, "Dear God, bless little John. Help him sleep well, think of You and love You his whole life. Amen." This may also help comfort him as he falls asleep.

Scared at Night

It is common for a child to be frightened at night. Every parent deals with this differently. You might suggest the child say a prayer asking God or his guardian angel for help. (See the Guardian Angel Prayer in LEARNING ABOUT ANGELS.) A conversation may go like this:

"Mommy, I'm scared."

"Why? What's wrong?"

"I don't know. It's dark and someone is going to get me."

"Did you say a prayer?"

"No."

"Let's say a prayer... Dear God, please help me not be scared. Make whatever is scaring me go away. Thank you for a great day and help me have a great day tomorrow, too. Help me have fun when I go to my friend's and play with their puppy. Thank you for taking care of me. Help me sleep well tonight. I love You, Jesus. I love You, God. I love you, Mary. Amen... Okay, God will help you sleep a little better. I love you and God really loves you very much. Good night."

You will be surprised at how much you put your child at ease. You have changed his thoughts from fear to anticipation for tomorrow. And since you asked, God will help the child sleep. He will "take away" whatever was scaring your child! If a child is scared, it is not of God; in the name of God, any unclean spirit who scares your child is powerless!

Pray Throughout Your Day

Informal Prayer

Stimulate your child to think about God continually, recognizing Him in all you do throughout your day. This can be used in disciplining, thanksgiving and interacting with other children. You can bring Him into conversation while driving down the road, going on a walk or playing in the house. A few sample suggestions follow.

Discipline

Discipline and punishment, unfortunately, are necessary at times. However, you can turn these unhappy moments into opportunities for teaching your child about God, His love and His forgiveness. "You shouldn't push or hit other children. That does not make God happy" or "When you hit your friend, it hurts God because he's God's buddy just like you," or, "Tonight in our prayers we'll tell God we're sorry for making up a story that's not true because God knows what really happened and He doesn't like us to tell a lie."

Thanksgiving

"Thank you God for that great tree and letting me climb it," or "Thank you God for my friend," or "Thank you God for letting me help my Mom and Dad today because I know it makes them so happy."

Interacting with Other Children

"Dear God, help me share my toys," or "Thank God for letting my friend come over to play," or "Help me God to learn to play nicely with my friend."

Driving Down the Road

"Thank God for making these 'happy clouds' and not 'rain clouds' today so we can go the park," or (on hearing a siren or seeing an emergency vehicle) "Someone needs help and the fire truck is going to help. Oh, dear God, please help those people who are hurt or need help," or "Dear God, please help Grandma feel better because she's sick today," or "there's the hospital where they take sick people; dear God makes the people in the hospital feel better."

Going on a Walk

"Look at all the things God made the birds, grass, bugs and dogs. God made these things for you and me; to make us smile and be happy," or "Look at this funny leaf (clover)! One is for the Father, one is for the Son and this one is for the Holy Spirit. Amen!," or "Let's see who can get to that tree first. It is nice God gave us legs so we can run fast."

Night Time Examples

Many parents say the "sandman" came to visit at night and left "goo goo" in their child's eyes. How scary! A man came into the room at night? No wonder a child is frightened at night! Try this: "Your guardian angel came to visit and to check on you. Your guardian angel is one of God's most special friends who helps God take care of you. Your angel saw you sleeping and told God you were fine."

The possibilities and opportunities are countless! Looking for and thinking about God throughout your day will be rewarding and pleasing to your child, to you and to God, too! Don't be surprised if you become emotional as your own relationship with God continues to grow through these continual prayerful conversations. Be thankful!

Pray For Children

Your child, as well as all children of the world, need <u>your</u> prayers. Our Lady has asked all Mothers to pray for children, ALL children.

For Your Own Child

Pray for your own child constantly. Let him hear you praying to God. He will learn to know your love for him and for God.

> "Thank you, God, for lending me this precious soul. Help me make my child pleasing to you so he can spend eternity with You in Your Kingdom."

"Let him love You, honor You, and worship You his entire life."

"Help our family imitate the Holy Family in our day to day life, especially in our obedience and love for You."

"Help me be more like Mary, Our Blessed Mother. Let me love and teach my child the way She loved and taught Jesus when He was young. She's my perfect example!"

Constantly offer prayers such as these for your child. Offer your day for him before your feet hit the floor in the morning. Ask for Mary's help. She will help you become efficient and motivated in your daily duties. Continually sacrifice and offer your daily duties such as laundry, cleaning and cooking for your child. Pray driving to the grocery store, playing games with your child or changing a diaper. Pray anytime! Do this especially when you are tired. Your reward will be great!

Bless Your Child
Bless your child. Bless him often. Use holy water, if you have some. If you do not have it in your home, it should be available from your church. If not, take some water to your priest and ask him to bless it. Bless him when he is quiet or when you are rocking him, holding him or kissing him good night. Make a small cross on his forehead with your thumb. "May God the Father, Son and Holy Spirit bless you, take care of you and help you every day."

For All Children
There are millions and millions of children who need prayers. There can never be too many prayers for children. Prayers never go unheard! Our Lady has asked mothers to continually include in their prayers:

Children whose parents, siblings and/or other role models are leading them astray by a poor example.

Children who do not know God.

Children who do not have parents.

Children who are aborted.

Children who are hungry, naked and/or homeless.

Children who are abused, physically and/or mentally.

Children who are neglected.

Children who are ill, especially the seriously ill.

Children who are handicapped and their families.

All children, including yours.

All families that they may live in peace.

For Your Child's Future

Pray for your child's future. God knows all, He knows the people who will be crossing your child's path tomorrow. Pray for your child's future teachers and playmates.

Pray that your child be receptive and excited about the places he will go. If he is to be a doctor or a nurse, let him be receptive and excited about science now. If he is to be an accountant or bookkeeper, let him excel in math now. If he is to be a spouse, parent, or religious, pray for him in this vocation also. Whether his duties be professional, spiritual or otherwise, lay a good foundation early so he will be good in his vocation later.

Pray for your child's future spouse. Pray that your child's spouse be kept holy and pure. Pray that his parents are teaching him of the Lord. Pray that his parents are setting a good example of a holy marriage.

If it's God's Will that your child be a priest or nun, pray that your child hears His call and responds quickly, boldly, with humility and sincerity.

Chapter 3

Let the children come to me and do not hinder them. It is to just such as these that the Kingdom of God belongs. I assure you whoever does not accept the reign of God like a little child shall not take part in it. (Mark 10:14-15)

Let The Children Come to Me

With a request like this from the Divine, we must baptize our child and take him to Mass on a regular basis.

Baptism

Besides being freed from original sin, baptism grants God's grace to a person. It also initiates the person into a lifelong membership in the Christian family.

In baptism, you (the parent) bless the child, profess your faith and agree to raise your child Catholic. You promise to be a good, Christian example, provide spiritual support and offer religious education for your child.

Most baptisms are a formal ceremony, administered by a priest. However, anyone may baptize at any time if there is danger of death. Relatives have been known to baptize children if they know the parents will not. Still it's best if performed by a priest.

To formally baptize your child, you must attend an orientation session at the parish where you are registered. Then, schedule the ceremony with your parish office or priest.

You must also select godparents. The Church requires one, and strongly suggests both godparents be baptized, practicing Catholics who regularly receive the Holy Eucharist. They are representatives of the Christian community. They can teach and guide your child and/or provide support through your child's upbringing. It would be nice, although not required, if the godparent is aware of and participates in important milestones in the Catholic development of your child, including First Holy Communion, Penance and Confirmation.

Baptism is a celebration of the beginning of new life. Celebrate!

You can invite family and friends to the baptism or "christening." Have a simple reception at the church or in your home. Include the priest with your other guests. You may also give small religious gifts to the child, such as a small crucifix or medallion or a statue of Jesus.

Giving a small gift to a friend's child who is baptized is not only a nice gesture, but an outward sign of your support and love in the Christian community.

Baptism is special; it is a once in a lifetime invitation into the Church, the Body of Christ, our community of faith. Make it special for your child.

Take Your Child to Mass

Taking your child to Mass does not mean taking him to the nursery or the cry room. It means taking him into the Church, before the Blessed Sacrament, seated relatively close where he can see what is occurring.

Begin when he is born! Attend Mass as a family, both parents, all kids. This may mean sacrifices, such as attending Mass twice because you have to be Eucharist minister or sing in the choir at a Mass that during nap time. Family Mass attendance is essential. It will set a good example.

Dress appropriately for Mass. Do not wear your blue jeans or shorts simply because you've been dressed up all week. Instead, dress up for God, do not dress down! You are on holy ground! Dress your child nicely, too! Make this a special day!

If the child is toilet trained, make sure you take him to the bathroom before you leave home. Convince him that leaving Mass to go to the rest room is not an option. You know that at times this is impossible. However, you can usually tell when there is a real need. Not him complaining "he's got to go!" after seeing another child leave Mass. You control the situation. Otherwise bad habits will be formed.

When entering church, allow the child to touch the holy water and cross himself. This can be done from the first day of his life. When he is newborn, you can cross and Bless him with holy water. He will eventually ask, "Why?" You can then explain that it reminds him of his baptism while he is saying "Hello" to God.

Before entering the pew, have your child genuflect <u>with you</u>. "Let's kneel down together to say 'Hello' to Jesus and let's tell Him we love Him." This may initially be a squat, possibly onto all fours. But it will eventually develop into a real genuflection. He will be participating, making God happy, and enjoying it. He may even want to go into the aisle several times during Mass just to genuflect. No harm done. As the child learns to talk, you can teach him to say, "My Lord and My God," as he genuflects out of love and reverence for God Himself present in the tabernacle.

While in church and talking about church and the Blessed Sacrament, use words like "reverence, adoration, and respect." These are big words, but they are important and your child will realize this from your attitude.

From the minute your child is born, let him participate in the Mass through your participation with him. Sing, respond to the readings and pray into his ear. Let him <u>hear</u> Mass through you. He loves your being close and snuggling anyhow. Do not deny him prayer.

Explain to your child the meaning of the symbols in church which make the Catholic church special. Start with the holy water. Point out the pictures and the statues of Jesus, Mary and Joseph. Look at the pictures in the stained glass. Identify the cross or crucifix. Comment on any pictures in the Missalette. Point to the Stations of the Cross, briefly explaining the steps of Jesus' Passion. See the banners used during the Paschal season. Look at the candles, choir, altar, tabernacle and baptistery. Teach your child to be observant and aware of the significance of the symbolism, colors, history and meaning of all the items in the church. Someday when your child visits a church of another faith, he may ask why you do not go there. You can refer to these many special items to help you answer his questions!

Perhaps he can wave hello and good-bye to Jesus on the cross, during the processional and recessional. Point out the activity taking place during the Mass. Let him hold song books and try to sing. This is fine, even if he can barely talk or hold the book alone. If he is small or does not become a distraction, he can stand on the pew while you hold his hand, perhaps dancing to the music. To God, this will be a prayer! Compliment him. He is participating and learning!

Make an effort to keep him from wiggling and being too noisy during the Liturgy of the Word. Explain that those people are "reading the Bible." Occasionally the reader will mention names such as Moses, Daniel or David, people he knows from reading the Children's Bible. If you bring a Children's Bible with you, you can quietly read parts of it. Do not get in a habit of reading to him during Mass! He can quietly thumb through the pictures by himself.

If you go to daily Mass, he can participate by carrying the gifts to the altar. The "Intentions" book is usually safe even if dropped, and he will be helping!

Allow him to put a few coins into the collection. Tell him that Father will give this money to poor people who do not have enough money to buy food or clothes. This is difficult for the child to understand, but less so than parish financing. It is a good time to learn that Jesus wants us to take care of others who need help. As the child gets older, teach him to set aside a portion of his allowance for the church collection. Teach him that God always keeps His promises, and He has told us that our blessing for being generous will be returned to us ten-fold.

Try desperately to keep him quiet during the Consecration of the Holy Eucharist and the Precious Blood. "This is the most special part of Mass. Be really still and watch Father ... see, he is holding the cup and the bread up to God in heaven, so, God will bless it and make it extra special for us. He turns it into Jesus; isn't that neat?" In a child's eye, this is exciting compared to reading and praying. Holding him close to you on the kneeler and whispering in his ear during this time will usually keep him calm. This also will discourage his crawling on the pew behind you and bothering other people nearby. If he continues wiggling, say "shhh, see all these other people are being quiet. They are on their knees saying prayers. So let's be really quiet so we won't bother them and maybe we can say some prayers, too."

Let him actively participate in the peace offering. He can do this with you and all the people around you. If he asks you what this means, tell him "you want all these people to be happy because they love God." As he grows older, explain that you are offering them "Peace, God's Peace, because you are forgiving them their sins. If you forgive them on earth, God will be happy and forgive them in heaven, too."

Take your child with you to the front of church when you
receive Holy Communion. Leave toys and books behind
and fold his hands together in prayer. Take the pacifier out
and keep it in your pocket for emergency! If you can hold
him, you can even whisper prayers in his ear as you move
towards the altar. He will want to receive Communion too,
and this can be difficult. But he will be cultivating a burn-
ing desire to receive Our Lord! If only more grown ups had
this yearning! As the child gets older he can begin to develop the habit of praying the Act of Contrition as he approaches Reception of the Eucharist. When it is time for
your child to receive his First Communion, a new prayer to
learn should be a Thanksgiving Prayer <u>after</u> communion!
(See FAVORITE CATHOLIC PRAYERS in the back pages
of the book for these prayers.)

A few more tips:

> Whisper prayers in his ear similar to your nightly prayers
> at appropriate times during the Mass. He can join with
> you if he likes.

> Take religious toys to Mass rather than secular toys. "We
> are going to God's house, so let's take this small statue
> of Jesus and Mary or your rosary to play with, and of
> course the Bible." Holy cards make nice church "toys"
> also. Cars, dolls and dinosaurs may sneak in, but hide
> them or replace them with others if possible. Do what
> you can to prevent the child's mind from wandering from
> what is important during this hour.

> Bribery, or "positive motivation," works too. Anyone
> who tells you otherwise probably does not have chil-
> dren! If you are having behavior problems with your
> child, tell him there will be no donuts after church.
> Perhaps "we can't go to Grandma's today unless you start
> acting nice while we are in church," or "if you are good,
> we can go to McDonald's after church." This is better

than leaving for the cry room every time your child acts up. If you leave, he will soon learn he can manipulate you and avoid church by misbehaving. Remember, this is a last resort for poor behavior, not a routine punishment.

There are times when a child cannot help the way he is acting. He truly bothers people around you. This is often predictable. His activities during the 24 hours prior to Mass may have caused it. Did he have a bad night? Did he miss his nap yesterday? Is he hungry? Did you rush out, missing breakfast? Is it 6:30 P.M. Mass on a holy day, so he missed dinner? Only you can be the judge of this. As long as <u>you</u> control when you take your child to the cry room, he does not manipulate you!

Attending Mass must be a pleasant experience. Remember this is a child. You cannot expect adult behavior. However, be careful not to over discipline, or it will become a dreaded hour. Discipline with love. Use hugs; spankings only make him more angry and cry louder. Compliment, praise and reward his good behavior. Express your pride each Sunday, reconfirming his good behavior. It can be fun and he is bombarded with affection for being good, he may even want to come back next week and be good!

You pray too! Make a special effort to pray during Mass. Not only will you set an example, but God will bless you! Never doubt, however, that you will be blessed just for getting to Mass! God accepts your sacrifice and understands the effort you made to get there! Just going is a prayer unto itself.

On Sundays when your child says, and really means, "I don't want to go to church today". Your reply can be simple and unarguable, "Sweetheart, it's one of God's main rules He gave to Moses. We have to go to church on Sundays and say our prayers. Everyone in church is a family of people whom all love God. This is the special day we pray together with this big family. Then we can come home and play". Then continue getting ready for Mass and change the topic of conversation.

Begin your own family tradition that makes Sundays special. Sunday is the day we celebrate Jesus' rising from the dead. Only God can do that, and we want to praise God for that! Do something in addition to Mass, which can be a visible sign to your child that this day is special. For example, use china at your main meal. Light a candle and say a special prayer at mealtime. Gather <u>as a family</u> to read a few stories from the Bible during the day. Pray a family rosary on Sunday. Be creative and think of something that you and your child will enjoy.

There may be a time when inappropriate behavior persists. The thought of the nursery sounds terrific. Take your protesting child to the nursery. On the walk, tell him "if you can't be good in church and sit still and listen, then you can't stay with me. You'll have to go with the baby-sitters." He will become angry. Next time he acts up, this will be an effective threat.

Ask for help from your guardian angel and from your child's guardian angel. Angels love to glorify God. They will offer help when asked, "Dear angel, please help guide my child to our Lord. Help his behavior be such to praise God".

Taking your child to Mass will become a joy, an absolute pleasure! It should be an integral part of your lives. You will watch your child develop and grow in his religion and his faith as he begins participating.

Church, Church Activities and Philanthropies

Teach your child the name of your church. Teach him to recognize it from the street, always pointing it out as you drive past. Also, teach him to bow his head or make the sign of the cross as you drive past out of respect and reverence for Jesus present in the tabernacle.

Become involved in church activities, especially community service work. Include your child in your efforts whenever possible. Find a niche that interests you, that you enjoy and that is of service to others. Then let your child tag along.

Become involved in children's education. If there is not a class for children younger than Pre-K, you may want to start one. You could start a "play group" for mothers and their young tots.

Work on meal preparations for the poor and the sick in your parish, or for those with new babies. Attend pro-life rallies, nursing home parties or visits. Deliver food or clothing donations. Visit and take some cookies to a grandparent or lonely neighbor.

Visit your church often, not just for Mass. There are dozens of reasons to stop by church for a minute. Drop off food for the poor pantry. Sign up for helping with an upcoming event. Attend daily Mass. Make a "poor box" donation, letting your child make the donation. Leave something in the office. Bring your child with you for all of these things! Explain that what you are doing is helping people. Helping people really makes God and Jesus happy. Thank your child for being such a big help! As your child gets older, you can explain that these acts are corporal works of mercy. By physically doing these acts of kindness we are expressing Jesus' love to those Jesus loves.

Be involved in all the church socials to which children are invited, including dances, ice cream socials, picnics and guest speakers. Let your child develop friendly relationships with other children and grown-ups of all ages from your parish. These relationships are healthy and fun. As your child grows older, encourage him to be involved as much as possible. He can be an altar server, attend Sunday school and help you prepare for church activities.

Finally, the most important part! Stop by the empty church to visit the Blessed Sacrament. Do it alone with your child! Cross yourselves with holy water, genuflect towards the Blessed Sacrament; then spend quality time with Our Lord. You can even sit on the floor near the altar. The child can say "Hello" and "Good bye" to Jesus on the crucifix. Suggest he say some prayers with you. You can sing "Jesus Loves Me," or "Away in a Manger." You can identify the familiar things around the altar. Point out the things which make your church, the Catholic Church, special. You can do it more leisurely than you can at Mass as described earlier. Do this often, explaining how special your church really is. Also, teach him to respect the sanctuary. The altar is holy ground. Running, jumping, and rolling around are not acceptable!

Find the statue of Our Lady and pray the "Hail Mary."

Look for the special intention candles. Light one and say a prayer. You can also follow the Stations of the Cross, which you have previously pointed to during Mass. These can briefly be explained such as, "Look, Jesus fell down because He is tired. That nice man is helping Him." or "See how that nice lady wiped Jesus' face when He was hot?" This can be a great learning experience. As the child gets older you can say the Stations of the Cross. This takes only 10 or 15 minutes and it should especially be done on Fridays.

Be prayerful! Thank God for your beautiful child. Ask Him to open your child's heart to love Him more and more.

If an opportunity arises to be in a Church of another denomination, point out what is missing. The explanation will help the child understand and appreciate all the Catholic Church offers.

Taking Your Child to Funerals

Many parents fear taking young children to funerals. The common reason is that he is too young to understand death. First, who really understands death? Second, do the parents fear the questions the child will ask and feel insecure of the proper answer? Both are common concerns. However, death is part of life. It is an issue which must be faced.

The decision whether or not to take a young child to a funeral can be difficult. You know your child best and you will have to decide when you can handle the funeral experience with him. A two-year-old may be totally oblivious to the situation. A three-year-old may be ready and able to handle the funeral. When between two and three does this maturity occur? Only you know the spiritual maturity of your child.

If possible, take your child first to a Catholic funeral Mass of a distant relative or friend. Hopefully you can do this before a close relative dies. He most likely will not have been really well acquainted with the deceased. But there will be many relatives or acquaintances there whom he will know. This is good.

Do not force it upon your child, but do not avoid the open casket. It is much easier to explain than a closed casket. Explain that "this person got really sick and died." Have your child feel his own heart. "See? You are alive! But this person's heart has stopped, so he cannot wake up and move around any more. It is really sad and we will miss him because we love him very much. That's why we don't play 'dead' with guns and swords-because it makes us sad. But do you know what? God is so happy and excited because this person has gone to be with Him in Heaven. How does that happen? His soul went to be with Jesus. It's gone and his body is left here. Close your eyes and pretend like you see Jesus ... doesn't that make you happy? That person is really happy too because his eyes are closed and he is with Jesus." If your child asks: When can I see Jesus? "Well, hopefully not for a long time. God wants us to live, so you don't have to worry about dying. I would really miss you if you go right now. So maybe you can wait a while, okay?" As your child gets a little older, maybe four or five years old, you can explain the soul.

Answer questions spontaneously. Watch your child's face for curious looks and draw any questions out. Do not leave him confused or afraid. Remember that your child still trusts you and believes whatever you say! Sound believable in your answers. Respond as best you can, simply and briefly. If you don't know the answer to a question, don't hesitate to ask someone!

He will probably do surprisingly well at the funeral Mass and the graveside service. Since you attend Mass regularly, there will be many similarities. Be open to questions any time that evening, the next day or weeks following the funeral. Answer them as best you can! There will be much learning and growth from the experience!

Remember, family is around to help. Recognize that death is part of life and can't be ignored! Finally, ask God to help you before you ever walk into the church! Ask Him to help you if you get a really tough question. Thank Him for allowing you this opportunity to teach your child more about Him. And when it's all over, thank Him again for not leaving your side throughout the funeral!

Taking Your Child to Confession
Take your child with you when you make your Confession. He need not go into the confessional with you. But if no one is present to help you, the priest will probably give you an extra blessing for bringing him along!

The message to teach your child is the importance of saying "I'm sorry." God already knows each of our sins and He loves us. But confessing them to a priest, allows us to examine our conscience, express our sorrow, receive God's grace and cleansing. It also brings us closer to God and those in our church. "We always want to make God happy. But sometimes we make mistakes. We sin. When we sin we make God sad. So we go and tell the priest we're sorry, and God tells the priest to tell us that He loves us very much." Use this opportunity to teach your child to say "I'm sorry" to kids or friends that he may have hurt. This is an important, often overlooked courtesy. Your child will learn and grow from this experience!

Your Priest, Your Friend

Get acquainted with your parish priest. Become his friend. This is possible even in a very large parish!

Do what you need to do for your child to know the priest. This may mean going to daily Mass, socializing after Mass for a length of time, or spending time at the church during a weekday.

If necessary ask the priest for an appointment. Invite him to your home for dinner. He may put you off because of a busy schedule, but if you continue to ask, he will respond.

This personal relationship is so important. Priests are descendants from the Apostles and Saint Peter, the Rock on Whom Christ founded His Church! These are Our Lady's beloved! Never speak ill of them and always keep them in your prayers! Visit them. Let them know you appreciate their work. Remember them on holidays and Holy Days. Teach your child that priests are very special friends of God. They do God's work all the time. They help us and teach us to do God's work, too.

Then pray, "Dear Lord, if you want my child to serve you by a call to religious life, so be it. Help him to hear and answer Your call. Always Lord, Your Will be done. Amen."

Chapter 4

Scriptures, the source of the wisdom which through faith in Jesus Christ leads to salvation. All Scripture is inspired by God and is useful for teaching, reproof, correction , and training in holiness so that the man of God may be fully equipped for every good work. (2 Timothy 3:15-17)

Learning Tools

Learning Through Hearing and Seeing

Books
Bibles: Most children love to have you read to them. Before they are six months old, they are intrigued with a colorful picture. Also, the quiet, uninterrupted reading time with you is recognized and loved by your child.

The Bible is a collection of stories inspired by God. There is a wide variety of children's Bibles available. It is probably good to have two or three in your home, especially if you have two or three children! Have at least one Bible with realistic pictures; others can have animated pictures. These will be available at Catholic book stores, Christian book stores, gift stores and sometimes even in secular book stores.

If at all possible, read the Bible at least every day. Bedtime is always good because you have fewer distractions. Your child will go to sleep thinking about God! It's also good to read the Bible throughout the day along with the many other books you read. It is fine if your child finds a favorite story and wants to read it over and over. As questions arise emphasize that the people and stories in the Bible were real, not imaginary. These were real people who loved and lived for God. This makes the Bible different and more special than any other story book.

Because of the variety of stories and characters, this may become your child's favorite storybook!

Store the Bibles with your other children's books. You may want them a little to the side, but do not put them high on a shelf restricting them for special times. Any time your child picks up the Bible and flips through the pages it becomes a special time. The more it is available and visible to him, the more he will read it. What a prayer in itself!

Children's Religious Books: Children love books and learn so much from them. Make religious books available to your child. Read to him often. Purchase books of short stories for children which have hard, laminated covers. Frequently the pages are hard as well. These can be read to children younger than one year of age. Read books about saying prayers and things God made. Find books containing simple, colorful and animated religious poems.

Exciting characters, good and bad, are in both the Old and New Testaments. Thrilling plots and colorful story lines can be found. Read about Moses both as a baby and as a man. Daniel in the Lion's Den, Adam and Eve, David and Goliath, Noah and the Ark and more can be found in the Old Testament. The New Testament has numerous stories and events from the Life of Jesus beginning with the Christmas Story and ending with the Ascension. Jesus' parables such as the Prodigal Son, the Lame Man who could walk and the Good Samaritan make great stories in and of themselves.

Keep these books in a special area with the children's Bibles. Make sure your child can reach them and look through them at any time. Read the stories over and over. Make them come alive the same way you would Mother Goose! It will help your child enjoy them enough to want to search for them next time he wants to read.

Often these books will be spread out all over the floor. Sometimes pages are torn. As long as they are well used, be happy. Thank God for His work in the mind and heart of your precious little one!

Adult Religious Books-Pretty Pictures: There are great religious books for adults which have large colored pictures. One adult book shows beautiful paintings of each of the mysteries of the rosary. Colored pictures are in the middle of many adult Bibles and in books about the saints. Watch for them in the bookstores. Keep these by your bed, or in another important, easily accessible place in your home.

Sometime, when your child is with you near the book, pick it up and look at the pictures. Tell him what is happening in a chronological, storybook fashion. Tell him about the saints and how special they are because they loved God so much. This spontaneous "reading" will be fun and different. You may find yourself "reading" the same books over and over. One day the child will begin to "read" it to you!

Audio and Video Tapes
Both audio and video tapes on religious themes are available. They may be more difficult to find, but it is worth the effort to find them.

If a Catholic bookstore does not carry these for children, or if their choices are limited, ask for catalogs. Also, check the Christian book store in your area.

Audio: Religious audio tapes should become an automatic part of your drives in the car. The radio has very little worth listening to for yourself, let alone your child. He will not be able to understand or relate to even a Christian radio station.

Play tapes with children's Bible songs. Find tapes with Old and New Testament stories. Your child will more than likely become fascinated with what happens next in the plot just as he does with secular tapes. You may even have to wait until it's over at the end of a car ride before leaving the car.

Video: Religious video tapes are much more difficult to find, but they are available. Many are only 30-45 minutes in length. They can be enjoyed in short intervals throughout your day. Old and New Testament stories are available. You can also find stories on Our Blessed Mother, on various saints, and on apparitions such as Fatima and Lourdes. As with any video, preview it before showing your child, checking for accuracy and appropriateness.

Having several of these available is terrific. Again, the child will become excited and entertained by the story (See the BIBLIOGRAPHY in the back of the book).

Listening and watching the picture books, videos and audio tapes throughout the day will help your child to grow and learn in the Spirit of God. God will become entrenched in his subconscious. He will be an important part of your child's life. How wonderful!

Your child will not fully understand all of the nuances of the theological, symbolical and other parallels and lessons of these stories. However, as he hears them throughout the years, he will find more and more meaning in the story line. Using

Noah as an example, a child's interest and ability to under-stand may occur like this:

Age 2: Interest in all the various animals

Age 2 1/2: It rained, and the animals were safe in the boat.

Age 3: Noah minded God, built a big boat to help save all of the animals. Obedience is very important to God!

Age 3 1/2: God put a rainbow in the sky because He was so happy Noah, his family and all the animals were safe.

Age 4: The dove brought back an olive branch, a sign of God's unending love, with hope and promise for new life and new land.

Age 5+: The importance of being good, obeying God, following His rules, the Ten Commandments. The con-sequences suffered from not minding God's Laws.

There are so many lessons to be learned! You will usually find more than one moral to each story in the Bible.

And an unexpected twist...your child may come to enjoy these favorites so much that he wants to share them with his friends. You may find your child explaining that Herod is the bad guy and the Three Kings are the good guys. You may be teaching other children and helping them grow in God too!

Singing
A child loves to sing. Singing makes him happy. It soothes him. Singing is also a form of prayer! Sing to him and sing with him often. Add religious songs to his repertoire.

When rocking your child to sleep, add "Jesus Loves Me" af-ter "Twinkle, Twinkle Little Star." At Christmas time, sing "Away in a Manger" or "Silent Night." These may become favorites and you will be requested to sing them into July! How beautiful!

Also, many tapes of children's Bible songs are available. Learn some of these and sing them at bedtime, too. Your child will enjoy the singing. God will enjoy hearing the prayers!

Learning Through Touch

Toy Religious Articles

A child, especially a young one (age one to three years old), learns the most about the world around him by touching and chewing on toys. Why not, then, allow him this freedom with toys representing the faith in which you had him baptized?

Buy him a 6"-8" statue of Jesus and Mary. Find him a wooden or cloth rosary which will not come apart at the chain links. At Christmas, find an inexpensive, non-breakable manger with which to play.

If it makes you more comfortable, do not have the articles blessed. You will feel less guilty if something happens to one, such as going down an elevator shaft or out a car window.

Teach your child to respect these toys above all others. He can hold it, chew on it, or play with it, but do not throw it across the room, jump on it, hit others with it or use it for a weapon! "This is Mary, Jesus' Mommy. Take care of Her so we make God happy. This is a rosary for saying prayers to God. It's okay to hold it, but please don't swing it or hit with it. It's for talking to God and it's special."

Store these toys in a special place. After all, they ARE special! They can sit on a shelf, on a kitchen cabinet or by the child's bed in a special, pre-determined spot. They could be kept on a small "altar" table in a special place in your home. Do not keep them out of reach. This defeats the purpose.

And do not throw them in the toy box with the dolls and race cars.

Allowing a child to familiarize himself with tangible images is important at this young age. It will help him recognize Jesus and Mary in other places in your home, in Church or in books and Bibles. Repetition with a variety of stimuli to all of his senses will serve to reinforce what you are teaching.

Religious Figures and Statues

Have religious statues and pictures throughout your home. Place a crucifix in a prominent location. Place another one in your bedroom. Each child should have his own crucifix for his room. If two kids share one room, that room may contain two crucifixes! Make sure each crucifix is blessed by a priest. Let the child be a part of this blessing.

Also, have a nice statue of Our Lady in your home. Keep Her in a special, visible place. There are also small, simple statues of the Holy Family, Jesus, Saint Joseph, the Way of the Cross, the Nativity and many, many more. You can continually add to your collection, sprinkling these throughout your home. Religious pictures should be used as well. Included among the most precious are that of Our Lord's Sacred Heart and the Immaculate Heart of Mary. Beautiful prayers and blessings are also available framed and ready for hanging in your home.

Begin when your child is an infant. Walk around and look at these pictures. If your baby is crying, show him the Sacred Heart, for example, say a little prayer asking Jesus to help your baby relax and rest.

Your child will see these articles day after day. They are visible reinforcements of what the child is hearing from you. They add substance to an otherwise intangible subject. It makes it easier to explain when they ask questions. Use them as a tool to help teach your child about Jesus, God and Mary.

Altar in Your Home
It is a nice idea to have a small altar in a prominent place in your home. This can be very simple, such as a small table with a cloth to cover. You can purchase inexpensive cotton cloth in paschal season colors such as purple, green, white, and red. You can keep small statues here such as a crucifix, Holy Family, Mother Mary. Pictures, such as the Sacred Heart could be displayed. Candles would also be a nice touch for family prayer. You could keep your rosaries here and gather for family prayer-time here.

Your altar should be at low-level so the child can see it. It could include Christian puzzles as well as non-breakable pictures, statues and rosaries.

Kissing Christ's Feet
Some children learn to give kisses before they can walk! This is how they first learn to say "I love you." Nothing is more delightful for a parent than when this happens for the first time. Would it not be delightful to Jesus also when He receives some kisses too?

As you carry your young child past your crucifix, stop to kiss Christ's feet. Say, "I love You." You must kiss Him too, as an example. This will be fun because kids love to give kisses, <u>AND</u> it makes Jesus "so happy when you kiss Him!"

As your child begins to walk, you may find him running to the crucifix all puckered up! It is a good idea to place the child's personal crucifix in his room at his level. Hang it just to the side and below the light switch. He can "kiss Jesus" when he wakes up and leaves his room in the morning, as he plays throughout the day and just before he turns out the light at night.

At times you will have to use gentle discipline explaining that "Jesus is so special and must stay hanging on the wall. You cannot take Him down and play with Him. He may break or get lost and that would be so sad. So let's put Jesus back up, Okay? Maybe we can find our little statue of Jesus to play with for a while."

Visiting playmates will probably become fascinated with the crucifix. They may never have seen one. If they have, it is out of their reach and far away. They become curious. Use this as an opportunity to teach them, too. Take advantage of having the attention of one of God's most precious souls! Teach them, too, that "Jesus is special. He loves you so much; that is why His arms are open wide to give you a big hug. You can kiss Him if you want. See, we like to kiss Jesus. Isn't that neat? It really makes God happy!"

Giving kisses is a child's way of expressing his love!

Holy Water Font
Place a plastic holy water font near the doors you most often use. Possibly your front and back doors. Hang it low so it is within children's reach. Begin developing a habit of blessing yourself and your children each time you leave your home. Blessings and graces will follow you as you as God accompanies you on your journey, no matter how brief. A priest will bless a gallon of water for you upon request. This simplifies keeping your font full, while allowing you to be generous with your blessings.

Stickers
Stickers are a favorite of almost every child. They love to stick them on paper, on their forehead, cheeks and clothes. Sometimes we find them on windows and walls! Inexpensive religious stickers are available in Catholic and Christian bookstores.

Allow your child to have a sheet or two on occasion. Use them to make pictures. He can stick them on pieces of construction paper. He can add to the art work by coloring with crayons or markers. This is a simple craft which will occupy him, in prayer, while thinking about Jesus.

Put his art work to good use. Use it for bookmarks for your Bible or other books. Hang it on the refrigerator at his level for him to admire. Hang it on the bulletin board in his room. Use it as a birthday card for family. Give it to a friend for a special occasion. Use your imagination with these pictures. Your child has laboriously produced them. Let it be his way of sharing and spreading the Good News!

Learning Through Play
Do you play house and act out Mom, Dad and child? Do you pretend to mow grass or cook on a camp out? Why not play games which will help teach the child about God?

Bible Stories
While out on a walk, find a stick. "Hey, let's play Moses...You be the king, I will be Moses...'Let my people go from Egypt to the promised land'...'no'...'then I will send frogs to hop in your hair and dinner...'" This can really be fun!

You can play Noah and the Ark with your stuffed animals or with plastic animals in the bathtub, combined with tug boats and Little People. Games and puzzles are available of Noah and the Ark.

Play and enact the stories which become your child's favorites as you read and reread the Bible.

Learning From the Saints
The ability to make, develop, nurture and encourage a relationship with a friend is a special gift from God. We share with a friend our sorrows and joys. We ask him for help and thank him when he supports us.

The Communion of Saints are special friends of God. They can become friends, confidants, helpers and great inspirations for you as well as your child. You must learn about them. You must put forth effort to develop a relationship with these friends.

The characteristic all saints have in common is their love for God. There are many, many stories about the saints, describing the lives they led and their devotion to God. Some stories are more animated, exciting and suited for children than others. Many saints were martyred. Your child will enjoy the story of their wholesome, devout lives.

You can find children's books and pamphlets about saints. Read a story to your child. Catholic book stores can provide information on the Saint's Feast Day in the Church. Methodically read about the entire host of saints or select a few favorites and learn more about them.

Once you familiarize yourself with the saints, pray to them asking for their intercession. For example, Saint Jude is the Patron Saint of Lost Causes and Impossible Situations. Pray to him, "Please ask God to help in this situation..." St. Anthony is the Patron Saint of Misplaced or Lost Articles, "St. Anthony, please help me find the pacifier!" St. Maria Goretti is the Patron Saint of boys and girls, that she might help them to be pure, "St. Maria Goretti, please help me be good to my friends. Help teach them about God." You can also teach them about their baptismal saint. They can re-light their baptismal candle as you teach them about the person after whom they were named. There are many, many more.

As a friend, each saint is a gift from God. They are present in heaven for you and your child for friends and examples. They do not diminish your prayer to the Holy Trinity or your devotion to Our Lady. They are helpful intercessors whom you are invited to know and to love. (See the FAVORITE CATHOLIC SAINTS section in the back of the book)

Learning About Angels

An angel is a pure spirit, created by God. God made them to help Him. Some serve Him by acting as messengers and guardians over people. We know this is true as angels are mentioned approximately 300 times in the Bible. Even Jesus referred to angels in the Garden of Gethsemane when He told Peter "I could call on all the Angels of Heaven to help Me if it was God's will". We believe each person has a guardian angel who prays for him, protects him and inspires him to do good.

Angels can seem scary. "Do they fly in my room and watch me at night?" Your terrified three year old may never fall asleep! It is essential to depict angels as very beautiful, peaceful, friendly and tangible. There is a picture called "The Guardian Angel" available through Catholic bookstores. This beautiful angel is watching carefully over a girl and boy as they play. Place this picture in your child's room. Suggest the child name their guardian angel.

You can teach your child to pray to his guardian angel. Ask favors. "Please ask God to help me fall asleep." In the morning and evening you can say the Guardian Angel prayer:

"Angel of God, my guardian dear, to whom God's love commits me here. Ever this day, (night), be at my side to light, to guard, to rule and guide. Amen."

Finally, you and your child can spend time looking for angels in your Children's Bible. You will find them in the Old Testament in such stories as Daniel and the Lion's Den and the Fiery Furnace. You will find them in the New Testament at the Annunciation when the angel, Gabriel told Mary about Jesus. At Christmas the host of angels appeared to the shepherd boys. And many Christmas cards portray beautiful angels with the Christ Child.

Angels are fun and exciting. Thank God for them!

Chapter 5

And I say to you, you are "Rock" and on this Rock I will build my Church, and the jaws of death shall not prevail against it... (Matthew 16:18)

Holy Days Of Obligation

Holy Days of Obligation are days we commemorate important events in the history of the Church. As Catholics, we are obligated to attend Mass on these days. Frequently they do not fall on Sundays. This is a great opportunity for you to teach your child. Here is a list of the Holy Days of obligation in chronological order by the Church calendar.

Immaculate Conception, December 8
Teach your child that Mary was conceived in the womb of her Mother, Anne, without Original Sin. She was, and is, perfect.

Christmas, December 25
We celebrate the Birthday of Jesus. More follows in this chapter on ways of celebrating Advent, the preparation for Christmas, and Christmas itself.

Solemnity of Mary, January 1
This is a day to honor Mary as the Mother of God. Explain to your child that Mary is an advocate for us to God the Father. We pray with her and ask her help and guidance.

She then asks God to hear and answer our prayers. Yes, God hears our prayers and can answer us directly. However, requesting Mary's assistance finds special favor with God as she is very, very special to Him.

Ascension Thursday, 40 Days After Easter

On this day we celebrate the rising of Jesus into Heaven in the presence of His apostles. This is often explained in the Easter books you read to your child. Also, every childrens' Bible has this story. Find it and read it to your child several times on Ascension Thursday.

Assumption, August 15

Mary was taken to heaven, body and soul and is celebrated on the feast of the Assumption. Although this will not be found in the children's Bible, it is pictured in Holy Rosary books. This is the fourth Glorious Mystery of the rosary. Tell your child that Jesus loved His Mom so much that He wanted Her in heaven right next to Him...and it's true!

All Saints Day, November 1

A saint is a person who died and is in heaven with God. This is the day we remember the saints. These people have set good examples on how to lead a Holy, Catholic life. Not <u>all</u> saints have been canonized by the Church. Was your mother or father a "saint?" Was a deceased friend a "saint?" Remember and pray for all souls who have died.

Chapter 6

Listen to my voice; then I will be your God and you shall be my people. Walk in all the ways that I command you, so that you may prosper. (Jeremiah 7:23)

Holy Seasons

Christmas
Christmas is the most exciting time of the year for most children. Parties, Santa, presents, candy and more fill the season. It is also an exciting time for the Church. The beginning of Advent is the beginning of the Church year. We celebrate the birth of Jesus! Teach this most important lesson to your child all through the season!

The Importance of Mary
Explain to your child that the angel Gabriel appeared to Mary and called her, "Hail Mary! Full of Grace! You have found favor with God! You will bear a Son and He shall be called Emmanuel, Jesus, the Son of God!" Tell your child: "How special and exciting this must have been for Mary. She was a <u>very</u> holy person. So God picked her especially to be Jesus' Mommy."

As children get older you can explain that Mary was the only person born without original sin. God prepared her to be the Mother of Jesus, perfect in every way.

It is also important that Mary obeyed. "She minded God." She said "yes" to God's Will. This is such an important lesson!

You can begin immediately talking about Christmas and its true meaning.

Advent

The beginning of Advent is the beginning of the Christmas season. Because retailers put Christmas displays up at Halloween does not mean you need to do the same. Just tell your child that it is not quite Christmas time. "After Thanksgiving, when we have the purple and pink candles in Church, we can get our Christmas things out and start getting ready for Jesus' birthday." Continually talk about "Jesus' birthday," rather than Santa or other secular traditions.

Advent Wreath/Chain/Calendar: The Advent Wreath is a lovely symbol of the preparation time before Christmas. It brings your family together, encourages prayer and escalates the anticipation for Jesus' birthday. It is a beautiful Catholic tradition which can be a great teaching tool for the entire family.

Each component of the wreath is symbolic. The circle means eternity and God's unending love. Tell your child "the circle goes around forever. God will love you forever too." The evergreen symbolizes everlasting life. "We can live with Him forever and ever!" Candles represent Jesus, the Light of the world. "The closer to His coming at Christmas, the brighter His light!"

As with any project, if your child can help arrange it, he will have more interest in its purpose and use.

Each time you sit down for a meal, light the appropriate number of candles and say a special prayer. This can be the Grace Before Meals, the O Jesus prayer mentioned earlier in this book, or weekly Advent prayers you will find in church or local Catholic bookstore.

The child won't want to wait until he finishes eating the meal to blow out the candles, but perhaps you can talk him into it! You may have to re-light them for each child to have a turn at blowing them out. It's okay if it's fun and prayerful!

Watch the Advent Wreath in your church very carefully. Each week a new candle is lit. You can compare this to your wreath at home. Tell your child each week that it's getting closer to Christmas. "When all four candles are lit, there are only a few more days left until Jesus' birthday."

Another easy Advent activity might be to make a paper chain with purple and pink links for each day during Advent and a Christmas symbol, such as a manger, at the end. Place this in a special place, perhaps by his bed or on the Christmas tree. He can take off one link each day. His excitement will heighten as he anticipates Jesus' birthday!   Also, this adds tangibility to an otherwise difficult to explain four week calendar.

Advent calendars are also fun. These are available in the stores. But you can make them at home. One type of calendar uses two pieces of construction paper or poster board. The top sheet has doors cut out which can be opened, one on each day of Advent. Behind the door is a small picture which is actually attached to the bottom sheet of paper in the area where it will be seen as the door is opened. Pictures could be simple Christmas and Christian symbols such as a candle, angel, advent wreath, star, manger, and shepherds. Each day your child opens a door and talks about the picture. You can also say a simple prayer at this time, developing an Advent ritual. When all the doors have been opened, it is Christmas Eve!

A second type of Advent calendar is a wall hanging consisting of a pocket for each day. A backing can be made of poster board, a large piece of felt or similar material. Small pockets can be sewn on or glued onto the backing. Prepare the calendar before Advent starts. Purchase a little treat for your child in each pocket. This gift could be a prayer card, a penny, candy, or a tree ornament. Each day of Advent the child removes a gift from a pocket. If you have more than one child, put one of the <u>same</u> gift in each pocket for each child to receive. When all the pockets are empty, it is Christmas Eve!

Look For Purple: While you are in Church, especially looking at the Advent Wreath, comment to your child about the use of purple. The candles and ribbons flowing from them will be purple. Father's vestments will be purple. banners and altar linens will be purple or decorated with purple ribbons.

Purple is a color the Church uses as a symbol of anticipation. Tell him "We're getting ready for Jesus' birthday! This is a time to get excited because something wonderful is about to happen. It's almost Jesus' birthday!" Purple is also a symbol of royalty, Jesus is our King of the World.

Manger Scenes: The manger is the most important Christmas decoration and a true symbol of Christmas. Your child can learn a great deal from having frequent, "hands on" access to a manger.

First, make him aware of the manger in your church. Go to the manger after Mass and look at it closely. Identify all of the characters. You can retell the Christmas story. Begin by pointing out the angel of the Lord. Notice that Jesus is missing because he has not been born yet and the three kings are missing because they come to visit Jesus after He is born. Then comment on the changes as the pieces are added.

Have <u>at least</u> one manger scene in your home that is nonbreakable and kept within the child's reach. It can be cloth, wood or plastic. They come in a variety of shapes and sizes.

Some may only have Mary, Joseph and Jesus while others have the entire collection of important characters.

Allow your child to touch and play with the characters. This does not mean he is allowed to throw them or use them as hockey pucks! Help your child arrange the shepherds and sheep. Carefully arrange the cows and donkeys, making the appropriate animal noises with each. Make this fun! The Christmas story will come alive in his heart and mind! Tell the Christmas story, adding the figures as they enter the story. This could become a fun nightly activity while preparing for Christmas.

Some suggest removing baby Jesus' throughout Advent and placing Him in the manger on Christmas Eve. This is a nice tradition, but it eliminates several weeks of "bonding" time for your child and the Infant. If given the opportunity, your child can become attached and relate to baby Jesus...care for Him, snuggle with Him and kiss Him.

Christmas Story Books: It is so easy to have several versions of the Christmas story available. Purchase some with realistic pictures and some that use cartoon style. Make sure the pictures are colorful and, preferably, keep the words simple.

Read these at least once a day. Depending on the book and the child's age who is hearing the story, you can simplify the book by "reading" the pictures, not the printed words. By the age of two, if you read the story often enough, the child may be able to "read" the pictures back to you!

Christmas Lights: When driving after dark, continually be aware of Christian symbols. Look for mangers, crosses and stars of Bethlehem. Point them out to your child and be excited about his discovery of new ones. Explain that people put up Christmas lights because lights are pretty and bright. People are excited about Jesus' birthday. Also, "Jesus was like a light. He made people shine with happiness. So we put up lights because we are happy to be thinking about Him and getting ready to have His birthday party!"

Santa Claus: There is nothing wrong with Santa being a part of the Christmas celebration. He cannot, however, be the main focal point throughout Advent. Simply tell your child who Santa Claus is: "A good friend of Jesus who makes children happy at Christmas by bringing them gifts." You can also talk about "St. Nicholas," especially on December 6, his feast day. He was a special friend of God, too, who did nice things for people. He became Santa Claus! Use the names interchangeably.

Some people elect to tell their child that Santa is make believe. He goes to the malls and parties, but no one sneaks into the house at night. Your child can enjoy the social events involving Santa, and you need not explain why each Santa looks different!

There is a terrific book entitled, *Santa and the Christ Child* by Nicholas Bakewell. This depicts Santa as special, and introduces boy Jesus who eventually takes Santa to the stable where He was born on the first Christmas. "Santa takes off his hat and kneels before an incredibly beautiful scene...the Nativity." This can become the child's favorite Christmas book.

Nativity Videos: Allow your child to watch a Nativity video he would enjoy. Repetition is important. He will learn to better distinguish the characters as they are brought to life. He will also experience the greatest joy of all when baby Jesus is Born! This video can be kept with all others and viewed year around.

Gift Giving: Place the emphasis on the giving of gifts as opposed to the getting. Do not continually ask your child, "What do you want for Christmas?" Place the emphasis on "What special present should we get for daddy or grandpa for Christmas?" Your child can prepare a "give" list as opposed to a "want" list. Then, let him shop with you. This may be slow, tiring and cumbersome. But this is the meaning of Christmas! God the Father gave His Son Jesus to the world; He was the Best Gift ever given!

A logical question: "If it's Jesus birthday, why are we buying presents for all these people?" A good answer might be "Jesus is up in heaven living with God. We can't really give Him presents. But if we think about Jesus, then we can make or buy a present for daddy. It really makes Jesus happy. We want Jesus to be happy. When we make others happy, He is happy. So we can buy a present or make a card for everyone who is special to us. When we see their happy face as we give it to them, we know Jesus and God are happy."

You might be surprised on Christmas morning when you awaken and your three year old says, "Oh Good! It's Christmas! Now I can give daddy his present and surprise him!" Oh the delight of Our Lord when our young loving and giving children learn about the true meaning of Christmas from you.

Christmas: "Happy Birthday Jesus!"

When you awaken, say, "This is Jesus birthday! Let's sing 'Happy Birthday' to Him before we open our presents!"

This will only take a few seconds. The child may already know the song; and of course it's very appropriate!

You can also sing "Happy Birthday" to Jesus before you dive into Christmas dinner. If you would like, put a candle on a food item such as the ham or desert. Since Jesus is in heaven with God, He would probably appreciate your child's help to blow out the candle! This will not only help your child, but may remind others present of the true meaning of Christmas!

Christmas Mass

Finally, and most importantly, take your child to Mass! This is essential as you celebrate what you've been talking about for 4 weeks! It will be so exciting to visit the manger which now places host to baby Jesus. Churches often do a good job of including children in their Christmas Liturgy. Allow your child to participate in whatever capacity he is invited. You could suggest a Christmas childrens' Mass to your pastor for Christmas Eve. Have a script for the Gospel. Older children could be key manger characters and the number of angel and shepherd participants could be unlimited. The younger children, ages 4 and under, could ring bells at specified times, such as when the angel says "Glory to God in the Highest..." Also during the Gloria! Your young child will delight in this participation.

Twelve Days of Christmas

The twelve days of Christmas begin December 26th and end January 6, the Feast of the Epiphany. Do something special each of these days with your family to remember Christmas.

Have a prayer time each day when you "Thank God for letting Jesus come to us at Christmas." Light a candle, then blow it out following the prayer. Plan to stop by church and visit the manger scene briefly on each of these days. Say "Thank you God for baby Jesus!" Stash some inexpensive baby gifts in your house. Have a baby bib, socks, bottles, pacifiers, formula and the like. If you have two kids, get 24 little gifts. Each day, after you say your prayer, have your child select a gift, wrap it if you would like, and place it in a pretty basket or decorated box. On January 6, take the box to an appropriate recipient, such as a home for unwed mothers or Catholic Charities. You can explain the relationship between your gift-giving and the Kings gift-giving to baby Jesus. How happy baby Jesus will be at this beautiful expression of love!

Epiphany

Although many people take down decorations, the Christmas Season does not actually end until the celebration of the feast of the Epiphany of the Lord on the Sunday nearest to January 6, the "twelfth day of Christmas." This feast celebrates the Magi's visit to the Holy Family with gifts of gold, frankincense and myrrh. These gifts help explain gift giving for Jesus' birthday.

You may want to leave your decorations out until then. If not, leave out at least one non-breakable Nativity set out until the Feast of the Epiphany. Let your child play with the Nativity set. Emphasize the three wise men visiting the baby Jesus.

You may have devoted a lot of time to Epiphany during Advent. If so, at least visit the manger in your church. Show your child what has happened. Explain that the church decorations will now be taken down.

Easter

Lent, Holy Week and Easter are by far the most important, special and significant time of the Liturgical year. They should be treated as such by your entire family.

Decorations: Hold off on your Easter decorations until Holy Saturday, after Good Friday. Lent is a solemn time. Your child can paint, color and decorate purple construction paper crosses to hang in the windows or on the refrigerator. A constant reminder of the season. Easter Eve (Holy Saturday) will be exciting. Decorate your house, color eggs, go on a hunt, be joyful! Then leave your decorations up for the Easter Season - the 40 days after Christ's resurrection until Ascension Thursday. Although this does not conform with society, it will make for a more meaningful Easter preparation.

Lent

Lent is a special time set aside by the church to help us focus on our journey to God. We should use this time to grow spiritually, and "get back on track" with our faith.

Lent prepares us for Easter with the use of prayer, fasting, penance and almsgiving. Holy Week begins with Palm Sunday and focuses on Holy Thursday (the Last Supper, including the Washing of Feet), Good Friday (the entire Passion: Agony in the Garden, Scourging at the Pillar, Crowning with Thorns, Carrying of the Cross—including Stations of the Cross—and the Crucifixion). Easter, the day Our Lord rose from the dead is, of course, the Grand Finale, the climax of 40 days of anticipation, the joy of our lives, the Resurrection!

Teach these things—all of them—to your child! This is the heart and soul of our Catholic Faith! It is so important the child learns this—all of it—at a young age!

Lent Suggestions: Make Lent special. This should be a time for spiritual growth for each family member and the family as a whole. Doing religious and spiritual activities with your child and family is one of the deepest intimacies and can be a bonding family experience. But this will not happen without preparation, thought and effort.

First, set attainable individual and family goals. What do you want to gain from Lent? Goals can be very simple, such as teaching your one-year-old to recognize Jesus on the cross or pictures of Mary, or perhaps teaching your three-year-old about almsgiving. Only you know the spiritual level and ability of your child. Do not underestimate him! He will anxiously anticipate Holy Week if you build his excitement for it. Also, do not ignore your own spiritual growth. Set goals to bring yourself closer to God. In this way, you can bring your family along too.

There are three main components in preparing for Easter: Prayer, Fasting, Almsgiving. Prayer is discussed in detail elsewhere in this book. Do not neglect making prayer important during Lent. Set a goal to learn a new prayer, pray for certain special intentions or pray a family rosary. It is a vital ingredient for you and your child's Easter preparation! Fasting is usually viewed as giving up food, such as chocolate or soda. But this does not have to be the case. You can fast from any earthly pleasure that is a sacrifice to you, such as no television or no telephone from 6-8 p.m. Offer this sacrifice cheerfully to God and use this time for spiritual growth (pray, read, family time). It will set an example for your child and will help you too. Your child can "fast" too, as you will see later in this chapter. Almsgiving usually suggests giving money to the poor. It could also consist of giving used clothing or other items, or charitable works donated to someone in need. Again, setting an example for your child is important.

Family Lenten Project: Make a large Lenten calendar for a prominent place, such as your refrigerator. Doing so will remind you of your plan. This should be at least the size of poster board. Butcher paper works well too. Since you are anticipating Easter, use purple markers and purple construction paper. Point this out to your child, too! Title the Calendar "Prayer, Fasting, Almsgiving ... Lent 199_ ."

Then plan something special for each of these components every day during Lent. Plan something for your child and something different for yourself. Put your intentions for the day on your calendar. Some suggestions might include:

Prayer: Select a daily prayer to say with your child. Find a special place to do this, such as on the floor near your calendar. This can be fun! Light a candle and say your prayer. This short prayer will be one he can learn and memorize during Lent. Learn a new prayer each year!

For yourself, select a different intention for each of the seven days of the week. Then, on each day, offer your sacrifice and prayers for this intention. For example: Sunday - End to Abortion; Monday - Peace in the World/Peace of Mind/Peace in the Family; Tuesday - Priests, that they pray the Rosary and remain holy; Wednesday - Family, your child, immediate family, Grandparents; Thursday - Praise and Thanksgiving for blessings; Friday - Passion, contemplate the Stations of the Cross; Saturday -Home, blessings and peace in your home and all other homes. Since there are seven weeks involved in Lent, you can also put each of the above seven prayer intentions down the left hand column on each Sunday. On the Lenten day, you then can go both up the column and across to find two special things to pray for. Another suggestion is to select a special intention and pray and fast fervently for this during Lent.

Fasting: Your child is too young to fast, or understand the purpose if you have him "give up" something. For example, abstaining from meat on Fridays may be something you do with him, and this is good. But he will not understand it's purpose when he is 1 - 4 years old! Try this: instead of "giving up" food for Lent, have him "give out" food. A lot of people do not have enough food and this is more tangible for your child to understand. Help your child decorate a good size box. Use paint, construction paper, markers or any fun medium. Then, purchase at least 40 non-perishable food items at the grocery store. Include a variety of items. You may need 40 items for each child, so think inexpensive! Then, prepare a special cabinet space near your other non-perishable foods to store these items. Following your daily morning prayer, let each child "pick out some food—only one" and put it in the box for the poor. When Lent is over you can then donate this box to a worthy cause. Your child can recognize the "fasting" or giving up food from his own cabinets as a sacrifice. What a great lesson!

As your child approaches age 5 you can add the true sacrifice dimension and help him give up something tangible, such as candy. "Jesus gave up His life, I can give up this piece of candy. I love you Lord, please hear my prayers." Just think how wonderful the basketful of candy will be on Easter morning.

Select a fasting sacrifice for yourself, as well. Offer up every temptation as a prayer for your child or for your personal intentions!

Almsgiving: Almsgiving consists of giving generously of your time, talent and treasure. This, too, is a very difficult concept for a young mind to understand.

> *Time:* Although this donation is for you or an older child, including the younger child is important. Time can be given by helping at church (office, cleaning, gardening, etc.), visiting elderly or sick or volunteering for your favorite charity. Offer your time doing these works of mercy as a gift to God. And take your child along. The elderly enjoy seeing children.

> *Talent:* Donating your talent can be fun and creative. If you are a good teacher, look for an opportunity to share knowledge. If you are good at arts and crafts, teach a class to elderly people or make items to donate. Maybe you are a good reader, spend time reading to your child's class. Find one of the special talents God gave you, and share it with someone during Lent and them offer it as a gift to God!

> *Treasure:* Playing with pennies is fun, and so is putting them in a piggy bank. So try combining the two. Almost every Church has Rice Bowls for Lent. These "piggy banks" for the poor are encouraged even for adults. Think of items in your home that you can count. Select something different every day of Lent and put this on your calendar. After placing the food in the

donation box, go see what we count today; then take your child and go count! For each item counted, give him a penny to put in the Rice Bowl. There can be 4 or 45 pennies each day. It can add up, especially if you have more than one child because each gets 45 pennies to add to the collection! After Easter, bring the Rice Bowl to Church and have your child give it to your Priest. Explain that Father will use this money to buy clothes for people who do not have enough money to buy their own. Father may purchase food, but this explanation is pretty close!

More than 40 examples of things to count in your home are: shoes in the closet, beds, windows, chairs, tables, pictures on walls, rooms, trees in yard, lights, wheels on cars, ABCs, tiles on kitchen floor, books on shelf, audio/video tapes, dishes in dishwasher, silverware in drawer, toys in bath tub, stairs, steps to mailbox, pages in newspaper, clocks, pictures/statues of Jesus/Mary, ceiling fans, closets, plates in cabinets, shirts in drawers, games in closet, keys on key ring, eyes/ears/noses/mouths in our family, pens in holder, fish in fish bowl, trash cans, radios/TVs, playing balls, coats/sweaters in closet, kitchen cabinets, days in Lent, eggs in refrigerator and anything else you can think of!

As your child gets older he can add part of his allowance to the collection.

Also giving of "treasure" does not have to be monetary. This is a good time to clean house! Not only are you preparing the way to Jesus' Resurrection, you can donate toys and clothes to a worthwhile organization. You can also purchase new items to donate!

You should also select an Almsgiving sacrifice for yourself. For example, take a donation to the poor box at Church 3 or 4 times a week. St. Vincent De Paul frequently has boxes too. Even though it may be small, this can be a humble and holy experience!

Family Lenten Project Suggestions: Holy Week should look a little different on your calendar. Maybe have some feet on Holy Thursday. Then tell your child the story of Jesus washing his apostles feet. On Good Friday, highlight with red marker or crayon telling your child This is the day we remember when Jesus died on the cross. You can also have a little picture of the crucifix in this square. You can find this on an inexpensive holy card. Put a huge, white Easter Lily picture on Easter Sunday, the day Jesus was Alive! You can even tape an artificial flower here! Throughout Lent, your child will anticipate Holy Week. When Holy Week comes, he will know something is special and different!

Mark off each day on your calendar as you do your prayer/fasting/almsgiving project. Your child could glue a purple cross made of construction paper to the day you marked off. This is fun for him and definitely marks the day!

A reduced sample of a Lenten family calendar is shown on the following page. This should be a fun daily practice. It will be a growing experience for your family. It will be an example and teaching tool for visitors in your home. Do not be shy or hesitant in explaining it to curious friends. You and your child will be touching others with Easter joy!

PRAY • FAST • GIVE ALMS

	SUNDAY	MONDAY	TUESDAY
SUMMARY **CHILD'S SACRIFICES** **PRAY** "Oh Jesus..." **FAST** Take one food item from cabinet for the poor each day. **ALMS** Count things daily for penny donation to rice bowl. **PARENT SACRIFICES** **PRAY** (Matrix exemplified) Intentions denoted by ✞. **FAST** From earthly pleasure, not denoted on this example calendar. **ALMS** Saint Vincent DePaul (✝)donation given daily. An "excuse" to stop by church and the Blessed Sacrament. ✝ *Use a purple cross to mark off each day!*	Sunday Intention for Parent: ✞ *End to Abortion*	Monday Intention for Parent: ✞ *Peace* • World • Self • Family	Tuesday Intention for Parent: ✞ *Priests* • Their Holiness • They Pray the Rosary
	1st Week Intention for Parent: ✞ *Own Home/ End Abortion* • Blessings • Peace	**Children's Daily Prayer** "Oh Jesus, I give you today, all that I think and do and say. Oh Mary, I love You & pray, more love today than yesterday. Oh God, be with me today. Be by my side forever to stay. Amen"	
	2nd Week Intention for Parent: ✞ *Praise/End Abortion* • Thanksgiving • Joy ✝ Alms: Chairs	Alms: Tables ✝ ✞ *Praise/Peace*	Alms: Pictures on Walls ✝ ✞ *Praise/Priests*
	3rd Week Intention for Parent: ✞ *Family/End Abortion* • Children ✝ • Immediate • Special Alms: Tiles in front Entry	Alms: Books in Child's Room ✝ ✞ *Family/Peace*	Alms: Tapes in Case ✝ ✞ *Family/Priests*
	4th Week Intention for Parent: ✞ *Priests/End Abortion* • Their Holiness ✝ • They Pray the Rosary Alms: Steps to Mailbox	Alms: Pages in Newspaper ✝ ✞ *Priests/Peace*	Alms: Cups in Dishwasher ✝ ✞ *Priests/Priests*
	5th Week Intention for Parent: ✞ *Peace/End Abortion* • World • Self • Family ✝ Alms: Pictures on Bookshelves	Alms: Shirts in Drawers ✝ ✞ *Peace/Peace*	Alms: Games in Closet ✝ ✞ *Peace/Priests*
	6th Week Intention for Parent: ✞ *End Abortion* Alms: Eyes/Ears/Mouths in our Family ✝	Alms: Pens in Drawer ✝ ✞ *End Abortion/ Peace*	Alms: Fish in Fishtank ✝ ✞ *End Abortion/ Priests*
	7th Week Intention for Parent: ✞ *Passion 12-3* *Stations of the Cross* Alms: Coats & ✝ Sweaters in Closets	Alms: Kitchen Cabinets and Drawers ✝	Alms: Kids Videos We Have ✝

WEDNESDAY	THURSDAY	FRIDAY	SATURDAY
		LENTEN CALENDAR	
Wednesday Intention for Parent: ✝ _Family_ • _Children_ • _Immediate_ • _Special_	Thursday Intention for Parent: ✝ _Praise_ • _Thanksgiving_ • _Joy_	Friday Intention for Parent: ✝ _Passion 12-3_ _Stations of the Cross_	Saturday Intention for Parent: ✝ _Own Home_ • _Blessings_ • _Peace_
Ash Wednesday • Fast & Abstinence Mass 6:30 am - ✝ 6:30 pm Alms: Shoes ✝ _Own Home/Family_	Alms: Beds & Pillows ✝ ✝ _Own Home/Praise_	Alms: Windows ✝ ✝ _Own Home/Passion_	Alms: Doors Confession 3:30 ✝ ✝ _Own Home/Own Home_
Alms: Rooms in House ✝ ✝ _Praise/Family_	Alms: Lights in House ✝ ✝ _Praise/Praise_	Alms: Toys in Bathtub ✝ ✝ _Praise/Passion_	Alms: Stairs in our House Confession 3:30 ✝ ✝ _Praise/Own Home_
Alms: Dishes used for Dinner ✝ ✝ _Family/Family_	Alms: Spoons in Drawer ✝ ✝ _Family/Praise_	Alms: Wheels on our Car ✝ ✝ _Family/Passion_	Alms: ABC's Confession 3:30 ✝ _Family/Own Home_
Alms: Clocks ✝ ✝ _Priests/Family_	Alms: Pictures/Statues of Jesus ✝ ✝ _Priests/Family_	Alms: Ceiling Fans ✝ ✝ _Priests/Passion_	Alms: Plates in Cabinet Confession 3:30 ✝ _Priests/Own Home_
Alms: Letters in Mailbox ✝ ✝ _Peace/Family_	Alms: Flowers in Flowerbed ✝ ✝ _Peace/Praise_	Alms: Closets ✝ ✝ _Peace/Passion_	Alms: Keys on Ring Confession 3:30 ✝ ✝ _Peace/Own Home_
Alms: Trash Cans ✝ ✝ _End Abortion/Family_	Alms: Napkins in Drawer ✝ ✝ _End Abortion/Praise_	Alms: Playing Balls ✝ ✝ _End Abortion/Passion_	Alms: Pictures/Statues of Mary Confession 3:30 ✝ _End Abortion/_ ✝ _Own Home_
Alms: Trees in Yard ✝ ✝ _Passion/Family_	**HOLY THURSDAY** Alms: TV's and Radios Mass 7:00 pm ✝ _Passion/Praise_	**GOOD FRIDAY** Service: 7:00 pm _Fast_ ✝ _Abstinence_	Easter Vigil 8 pm

More Lenten Suggestions:

> Read the Easter Story to your child from a children's Bible frequently. Always begin with "Palm Sunday." Read all of the story, ending with the Resurrection or the Ascension. You will be ending the story on a good, happy note, not simply "Jesus Died on the Cross."

> Hide "Gloria" and "Alleluia". Help your child make a sign, poster or several small cards with the words "Gloria" and "Alleluia," which are not used at Mass throughout Lent. Then hide it for them in your home. Bring them out on Easter Sunday morning. This is a simple, fun and meaningful tradition.

Palm Sunday

Palm Sunday is celebrated on the Sunday before Easter. Explain: "This is the day Jesus rode into Jerusalem on a donkey. The people of the village waved palm branches. They spread the branches and some of their clothing on the ground for the donkey to walk on. This was a special carpet they made for Jesus because they knew He was special. They thought he would be their new King. But he was King of Heaven, not just their town."

Before Mass, everyone, including your child, will receive a palm branch to remind him of this parade. There will also be a procession in the Church. Encourage him to participate. This begins to elevate his anticipation for Holy Week. Your child may want to keep his palm branch. Keep it in a special place in his room, perhaps behind his crucifix, and it will be a visual reminder of this eventful celebration. Remember, it is blessed, so dispose of it properly (burn, bury or return to church).

You can also point out the absence of purple (waiting) and the presence of red (Jesus' blood, sacrifice). The priests' garments and the altar cloths will be red. We are no longer waiting, but remembering Jesus suffering and death.

Holy Week

Although these days are not Holy Days of Obligation for the Church, they are among the most Holy, important days of the Church year. We base our faith on what happens this week!

Take your child to Holy Thursday Mass and Good Friday services. He has been preparing for and anticipating these days for a long time. You have been telling him about washing feet, the Last Supper, the Crucifixion, kissing the Feet of Our Lord on His Cross for well over a month. Surely his curiosity and interest level is up. These services will be the best possible illustration for young children to understand Easter. Our Lord does not want to scare children, and the services are not scary. They are sad and solemn. They set a mood.

You will need to briefly explain what is happening. For example, "Father is washing the feet of twelve people to remind us how Jesus washed the feet of His twelve apostles." or, "Father is not doing the bread and wine tonight because Jesus isn't here. We do not have to kneel down (genuflect) because that (the tabernacle) is empty. Jesus is gone tonight. He died on the cross. It's so sad; that's why all the table cloths are put away and the pretty decorations are covered." Your child will surprise you. He will be quiet, attentive, sad.

Good Friday is Special

Do not treat Good Friday like any ordinary Friday. It is the day Our Lord suffered and died for us. Your home should reflect this extraordinary event. Unplug your television and radio for the day. Let it be a peaceful and prayerful day. Or spend the day watching a movie on the life of Christ.

Make an effort for you <u>and</u> your child to venerate the cross at 3 p.m. on Good Friday even if it is the one in your own home. It was the very hour of the death of Jesus. Try saying your rosary, contemplating the sorrowful mysteries. Have your child color pictures from a colorbook of the Way of the Cross. You can also go by church and mediate the Stations of the Cross while you are reflecting upon them too.

As your child gets older, take him out of school to commemorate this Most Holy Day of the year. This is valuable spiritual and family time. The Consummation of the Mission of Jesus, our God. Keep it Holy!

This is a very solemn, holy day!

Easter Sunday

While your child is very young, start Easter Day with a prayer. Begin a family tradition! As soon as your child wakes Easter morning, get down on your knees as a family. Thank Jesus for His suffering on the cross, but especially for being alive!

"Jesus is alive! Today is the day He rose from the dead! Isn't this a great day! We're so happy. Thank you God! We can get all dressed up in our new church clothes for Mass today!"

Only after you pray, should you look for eggs, eat candy and go to Mass! Arrive early so you can sit towards the front. Point out all the flowers and all the white. The red is gone! Easter is here and everyone is so happy! Look at the new clothes and the Easter hats. It is a time to celebrate!

Look for Easter symbols in your Church. The Easter lily represents beauty, perfection, goodness, joy and resurrection. It is shaped like a horn pointing to heaven, announcing the Good News! Light, such as the Easter candle, is a symbol of Christ's triumph over darkness.

It is okay to talk about the Easter bunny and hiding Easter eggs—the signs of new life. However, do not expect children to make much of a parallel between the secular and religious celebrations. This may even be hard for adults to explain! As long as your emphasis is teaching that the season is holy, you are doing well!

Have your child listen closely to the Gospel. It tells that Jesus is alive! Celebrate with Him and your family.

Easter Week

Easter is a season, not a day. Remind your child of the importance of this whole week. Talk about Jesus being alive! Perform acts of kindness to "make Jesus happy!" This could include returning your Rice Bowl to Church or delivering your fasting food collection to a worthy organization. You can gather around a new, white candle. It is different from the one you used during Lent. Say a "Thank you God for Jesus being alive" prayer. Your efforts do not have to be exaggerated, but recognizing this as a Holy Week is essential.

Ascension: As mentioned previously, this Holy Day of Obligation celebrates the Rising of Jesus into Heaven. This is the end of the Church's Easter Celebration. Now is a good time to put away Easter decorations.

Chapter 7

You were progressing so well; who diverted you from the path of truth? Such enticement does not come from Him who calls you...I trust that in the Lord, you will not adopt a different view. (Galatians 5:7-8, 10)

Secular Holidays

The word "holiday" comes from a combination of two words: "holy" and "day." Thus, almost every secular holiday has a holy or religious history, purpose or meaning. The secular world has changed the emphasis and celebration of some Church feasts. Halloween and to a lesser extent St. Patrick's Day are not the "Holy Days" of the Church. The religious origin has virtually been eliminated.

It would do more harm than good to isolate your child from society by not allowing him to participate in these non-Christian celebrations. He will eventually learn society's ways and celebrate the holidays in a pagan form.

Most every secular holiday can be given a religious explanation. However, the Christian stories of St. Valentines and St. Patrick will not be nearly as entertaining to your child as all the Valentines, candy and Wearin' of the Green!

Find simple activities and make simple explanations of the Holiness of the day. Bring God into the secular celebration!

Also, remember your priest on these holidays, especially Father's Day! Help your child make your priest a card, basket of candies, cookies, etc. What a nice gesture! Your priest will appreciate being remembered, and he will remember you!

The following are a few suggested ways you can handle these days:

Saint Valentine's Day (February 14)

Love is a special gift from God. On this day we tell about our love and show our love to our family and friends. Give lots of hugs and kisses on Valentines Day!

It would be good to tell your child that St. Valentine was a real person who taught people all around him how to love. Some people did not love God. They put Christians, like St. Valentine, in jail. But St. Valentine wrote letters to his friends about God's love, how to love and the importance of love. These were the first "love" notes, and led to the tradition of sending "Valentines" notes to those we love.

Plan a special family activity this day. It would be nice to have a romantic dinner with your spouse. But it will be equally special to have a "Love" meal with your family serving Roasted Love (roast beef), crushed love (mashed potatoes), United Love (peas and carrots), Red Rose (red jello), Dreamy Love (rolls), Golden Love (butter), Deep Love (chocolate dessert) and Warm Love (hot tea or coffee). This may seem silly, but it will be great fun. You can also read the parable, "The Good Samaritan." Talk about loving your neighbor as well as how Jesus loves everyone, especially children!

Another idea is to make Valentines with a "love" scripture verse (there are many!). "Love one another as I have loved you", "The greatest gift is love", "God so loved the world that he gave His only Begotten Son, that whoever believed in Him would not die, but have eternal life."

Saint Patrick's Day (March 17)

When your child gets older, you can discuss all the folklore and history involving St. Patrick and Ireland. But when he is young, he will only see all the green and the shamrocks. It is easy to point out the three leaves of the clover, telling your child they represent God the Father, Son and Holy Spirit! Look for clover throughout your day, and continue to talk of the Holy Trinity! This is a prayer in itself! Decorate your home with shamrocks the week before St. Patrick's Day. Cut them out of green construction paper and let your child paint, color, glitter or mosaic them. This is fun and you can talk about God all week in a new, refreshing way!

Mother's Day and Father's Day

When you attend Mass on these days, say extra special prayers for the mothers, grandmothers, fathers and grandfathers in your and your child's life. Help him make homemade cards for these special people. If possible spend those days with the mothers and fathers closest to you. Say "Thank you" prayers all day with your child. Also say simple prayers such as "Dear God, please help all mommies and daddies love their children." Remember your priest on Father's Day. He is the Father, the head of your Christian family.

Independence Day (July 4)

Thank God for His blessings on you and your family by letting you live in America. So many take advantage of this great gift! You can say prayers throughout the day with your child such as, "Thank you God for America. Thank you for letting me go to church whenever I want." Sing "God Bless America!"

Halloween (October 31)

Halloween has become a major holiday in America, a true victory for Satan. The word Halloween is actually "All Hallows Eve", the eve of All Saints Day. Early Christians would remember all who had died on this day. This included evil people too. So they carved the pumpkin, hoping it would keep away evil spirits. Other demonic traditions also crept in. This is the most "sacred" day for witches and devil worshippers. They gain more followers and offer more sacrifices on Halloween than any day of the year.

Deny Satan the recognition and satisfaction he wants by not celebrating his day and turning attention towards God.

Society has made Halloween fun and cute. Such are Satan's sneaky ways.

Your younger kids won't miss it. The costumes and candy are really for your pleasure, they get sucked into it. Your older kids can accept your explanation and will respect you for standing your ground with your beliefs. You will, however, be challenged by your kids. Be prepared to discuss it and don't give in!

Halloween Alternative: Fall Festival or All Saint's Party

Create your own tradition. Plan something really fun for the kids on the same evening others are Trick-or-Treating. Invite friends who share your beliefs. A Fall Festival Party could include: making caramel apples, bobbing for apples, pin the leaves on the trees, candy hunt (the favorite). You could prepare by decorating Fall leaves. You could also incorporate All Saints Day by making costumes representing a favorite Saint; coloring and hanging pictures from coloring books about Saints, available at Catholic Book Stores; watching a favorite Saint video for entertainment is also appropriate.

Thanksgiving

Although this feast is of American history and not of the Bible, it can be a very holy day. God wants us to be thankful for our many blessings. You can spend the entire day being thankful for everything from family and friends to nature such as animals, trees and flowers. Your child can be thankful for toys, Church and even Jesus and Mary! When you say your prayers, take turns with your child naming things to be thankful for. How many can you think of?

Chapter 8

But Peter and the apostles answering said: we ought to obey God rather than men. (Acts 5:29)

Controlling Your Child's Sensory Input

Your child's bright little mind is a blank slate continually bombarded with all types of stimulation. Some of it is good, some of it bad. He is not able to discern between real and pretend. To him it is all real. As a parent you must continually monitor what your child receives in his sensory input. You should constantly be aware of supposedly "good guy" cartoons, the evening news, the car radio, children's' books and toys, conversations with his playmates and inappropriate adult language and conversations. Do you really approve of all your child's intake? If not, eliminate it, especially while your child is very young. At least do your best to do so. It will be impossible to eliminate everything because the child plays, goes to school and spends time with other children who have been exposed to much more. You cannot raise your child in isolation, God does not expect you to. He does expect parents to be aware, and to control the message when you can. Christ tells us to be "in the world but not of the world."

It is absurd to think that your child cannot grasp the reality of God in three persons because God is intangible. Think of Ronald McDonald. Your child has probably never truly seen the <u>real</u> Ronald, but he believes in his existence. He's on TV. He is imprinted on his lunch tray, his toys, and anywhere else where he can sell hamburgers. If this can be reality to him, so can Jesus. With tangible stimulus, Jesus can be a reality for the very young.

Television

The average American has at least one television set in their home. And the average child watches television between four and six hours <u>each </u>day! This is sad but true.

As a parent, you must be very concerned about all the information your child absorbs from the TV. He does not even have to be watching it for the information to penetrate.

Following are some thoughts and suggestions for TV viewing in your home:

> Remember, you control your TV. You are in charge, you set the rules. Whatever you decide, your family must respect and follow. Do not let your child talk you into more TV than you want him to get! Set your rules while your child is still young. Some rules could include having him ask before turning on the TV. Turning it on is not an automatic reflex caused by walking into the room. Do not allow personal TVs in bedrooms. Not only can you not control what he is watching, but this leads to isolation from the family.

> Be a good example. Minimize your own viewing time. You may be surprised at how much time you spend glued to the tube! Set specific programs you want to see, then turn the TV off. Find an alternate activity. Remember, your actions and examples say more than your rules.

> Television is not a pacifier or free baby-sitter. Do not treat it as such. This is easy and convenient, yet it can be so harmful. For example, cartoons are on TV and it is

time to make dinner. So you leave your child and escape to the kitchen. Meanwhile, the cartoons end and the news comes on. "Oh well, it's just the news, what can be harmful about that"... only murder, rape, theft, deadly car crashes, politics and a host of other subjects not well-suited for a small child!!! Be alert. Either watch with him or know what is on every minute. If his show ends, encourage him to play. Suggest he help you with dinner. Minimize TV time!

Not allowing the TV to be baby-sitter creates more work, time and effort on your part. But remember your child and his moral and value development will be worth the trouble.

When your child does watch television, watch it with him on your lap and talk about what is happening as the story unfolds. Be ready to answer questions. Be ready to comment on poor language or poor decisions and actions by the characters. Express your negative reaction immediately. "That wasn't good for him to say that not nice word. Saying 'stupid' makes that person sad, and that doesn't make God happy." or "They shouldn't hit people like that/jump off of the building/etc. That's dangerous and can hurt you." If you become shocked or do not approve of the show, change the channel! Your child may object, but simply explain what is wrong and why you do not like it. This does not have to be a lengthy or complicated explanation. Just say, "let's find something funny instead of this sad show..."

Cartoons

Are Ninja Turtles and Power Rangers really good? Maybe they <u>are</u> the good guys in the show. Yet, children imitate them by swinging weapons and hitting or kicking other children. Is this of God? You probably grew up with a taste for a little violent cartoon watching. Who did not laugh as the Road Runner evaded Wiley E. Coyote and then the canine fell 3 miles to the bottom of the Grand Canyon? And Popeye popping a can of the green stuff and then stuffing Bluto!

But there is a world of difference between the cartoons you grew up with and the ones your child is exposed to today. Many cartoons today have references to mysticism, mind control, spiritism and universalism. Many talk about "the power of the force". *If you don't believe this, or believe it is an exaggeration turn on the TV and watch and decide for yourself!*

A recent example is the Mario Brothers rescuing the princess and trying to escape from the bad guys. The Princess and Mario come to a river and Mario raises a scepter-like stick and the river parts. The Christian term for this is "blasphemy." This was one of the most wonderful miracles God gives us in the Bible and it is reduced to a Nintendo trick! When your child grows up and learns about Moses parting the Red Sea, he will think—"Oh yeah! I've seen this before...Mario did that last week...big deal!"

As old fashioned as it sounds, evil can creep into your home and into your child's little mind via TV. Evil is subtle. If at age 2, 3 and 4 your child has seen mind control, mysticism, violence; if he-man has "the power," then how can your child recognize "The Power" of Jesus, the Prince of Peace, the Way, the Truth, and the Light, the King of Kings, our Lord and Savior? Do not diminish "The Power" of Jesus by exposing your child to a lot of the garbage shown on today's cartoons!

Much research has been done in the use of television to introduce and support negative influences on children. Many articles and books are available on this subject.
There are still good program choices. Nickelodeon, The Family Channel and Public Television offer a wide variety of good shows for all ages. Most children also love nature or discovery shows and most parents find them equally fascinating. Nature shows may prompt questions and conversa-

tion. Be prepared when some nature shows are a bit graphic about natures way!

Other popular TV choices for young children are old favorites like Sesame Street, Mr. Rogers, and Barney, which are always faithful to both child and parent with their simple yet fun lessons. They have given us years of enjoyment and education. Watch for TV Guide's annual rating of children's shows. It provides some valuable input.

To minimize the amount of TV viewing while simultaneously avoiding confrontation with a child old enough to tell time, have pre-determined viewing times. Generally, a child loves structure. It helps him feel in control of a world over which he does not have much control. Prepare a written schedule with times and activities (play time, homework, feed pets, set table for dinner, TV time and so forth).

Saturday Morning Blues

Are Saturday mornings a battle between you and your child over which cartoons to watch? If you have a VCR, tape several episodes of your child's favorite show (of which you approve). Your child will not feel cheated. You will have peace of mind and hopefully you will have avoided a confrontation every 30 minutes!

Does your child wake you early, especially on Saturday mornings, and want you to turn the cartoons on? Why not divert him from the inevitable? "Here, climb up in bed with me/us and let me kiss your cheek a minute, let me get your piggies warm or lets tickle daddy." Suggest something fun. Then hug, kiss, tickle, play with your child. Suggest you play board games or read books. This is a special Saturday morning treat not allowed during the week! This will be the best, undisturbed, quality time all weekend! Plus, you get to stay in bed an extra few minutes before turning on the TV!

Start a Saturday morning tradition that requires leaving the house and the TV. How about going out for donuts every Saturday morning. Dad could take him fishing or to McDonalds on Saturday mornings. Plan something fun to which both child and parent look forward. It can become a family tradition.

Family Activities - TV Alternatives

Family activities are a great alternative to watching television. It is no secret we sometimes get into a rut with family activities. It is easy to just flip on the tube. Following is a list of great family activities which are inexpensive, enhance family conversation and please God.

Try walking, bike riding, baking cookies together, going to the park or zoo, going on a picnic, doing arts and crafts, participating in church activities, reading books together, planning a one-day trip, fishing, feeding the ducks, doing yard work together, cleaning house or flying a kite. Go on nature walks and collect leaves, pine cones, and the like. Enjoy sports together—softball, putt-putt, Frisbee, golf, tennis. Spend reading time at the library. Plant flowers or a vegetable garden. Visit museums.

Books

What is your child looking at and reading about in his books? Do they have witches and terribly evil characters? Stories such as Snow White, Hansel and Gretel or Sleeping Beauty with their spells and witches are the worst!

There are thousands of books which do not involve these characters, spells and trances. Some good choices are Sesame Street Books, Bible Stories and informative books such as "All About Fire Trucks," " All About Animals," "All About Colors, Circus, Trains."

You must still review some of today's books. Some show the lead characters in Spiritism. Some levitate, stare into a floating crystal ball and project the future. Some go into a trance and give a crystal ball as a birthday present. At the age of 4 or 5 and younger, your child should not be exposed to levitating, trances and crystal balls, no matter how silly or insignificant it seems! Also, why read books whose characters call each other liars, even if in not so many words. Why select books that talk about stealing or who use words like "stupid," "dumb" and "kill." If the book is good except for a few words, change the words as you read!

You must be aware of what your child reads, but <u>do</u> encourage reading! Give books as presents. Make going to the library a tradition and a treat. Most public libraries have fun areas set up for children with puzzles and learning toys.

Check into story telling time at the library, where gifted librarians read to children accompanied by puppets and story boards. These story times usually are age specific. There is a time for 2-3 year olds and a time for 4-5 year olds. Each session has a topic such as bears, Valentines, zoos and the like. Story times are offered both during the day and in the evening. Maybe both Mom and Dad could go along!

As your child gets older previewing and screening books become more difficult and time-consuming. However, it also becomes more critical as the subject matter becomes more advanced. There are some scary, adult story lines camouflaged with children's book covers!

Toys

Control what your child plays with while you can! If you are not sure about something specific, ask yourself if you think God would like this, or if Mary would let little Jesus play with this toy or read this book? You will probably get your answer quickly!

What about weapons? This is especially true for boys. No wonder our jails are full of men. We raise boys with guns, swords, army men, hand cuffs and the list goes on. Eliminate these toys as much as possible, especially when the child is really young. You can slowly introduce them as he realizes they exist. He will see them at friends' houses. Explain, in private to your child why you do not really like the toy very much. Refer to specific situations which may have just occurred with the friend. Let them know they can be dangerous and hurt people.

Inevitably your child will come home from a birthday party with a questionable toy or gun and love it! Do not scold him. Talk with him about why you do not want him behaving like certain characters. Tell him not to point guns at people. Encourage conversation about the subject. If you do not discuss this with your child, he will participate and not tell you. Hiding his participation and lying to you can have terrible long-range effects.

As your child ages, you can introduce these characters and toys. Do it only when he can distinguish between appropriate and inappropriate behavior and when you can discipline him for misbehaving. Be consistent with your punishment when he does not follow your guidelines. You must punish pretending bad behavior because "someone will get hurt, and that would make God sad." Inevitably, someone <u>will</u> get hit or hurt with one of these toys. Jump on this opportunity to teach!

You may have to allow your older child to play with these toys or watch TV shows with questionable characters while your young child is asleep. Tell him your younger child cannot distinguish some of the issues until he is a little older. Your older child will feel grown up and important because of this privilege.

There is an endless list of toys that encourage positive behavior and help in learning. Just a few are Legos, wooden blocks, toy cars and trucks, balls, baby dolls, tea sets, puzzles, toy kitchens, work benches with tools.

When friends and family ask what to give your child for Christmas and birthdays, do not hesitate to tell them the toys that you have approved and the toys that do not have your approval!

Movies

Be extra careful about taking your child to the Big Screen. Even with adult movies, the ratings can be misleading. Some "G" movies contain scenes which may be scary to a 2-5 year old. Friendly monster adventures where the good guy wins can be really huge, loud, and intimidating in a theater. At least if you wait until these come out on video, the child has the safety and security of his own home and distractions such as favorite toys around in case he gets scared. Think about it, consider the delicate mind you are molding.

Also, many "children's" movies contain adult content and satanic undertones. Is the movie suitable for children if the animated characters were real actors? There are good movies, but it can be difficult finding them. One option is to wait until the movie comes out in video. Rent it, preview it for the kinds without them knowing it (so they won't nag!). Then make your decision on its appropriateness for your Godly children.

As your child gets older, you may allow him to see more movies. However, do not turn him loose! Preview the movie first, see it with him. If this is not possible, at least discuss the content with him.

When You are Not at Home

When you leave the house with the baby-sitter in charge, you will leave basic information such as the number where you will be, the doctor's number, bedtime, dinner and snack information. Do not assume baby-sitters or relatives know your house rules. It is your responsibility to explain house rules. Some examples you may already have or want to think about are:

No MTV.

No boyfriends (or girl friends).

No Movies, especially PG-13 or R-Rated.

No Cartoons and *only* TV programs you specify by name.

No Profanity.

No long telephone conversations.

To a 16 or 17 year old baby-sitter these may seem strict or "no big deal," but to a 2, 3, or 4 year old they are damaging. Just because you are not in the house does not mean you have to give up control of what your child hears and sees!

As your children get older, you can learn a lot from them. Ask them what the baby-sitter did. If it was watch TV, ask what shows. This can be invaluable information. Make sure your child understands his first loyalty - Mom and Dad. If the baby-sitter says, "don't tell your parents", then they are probably hiding something. It is your love for your child and God's help which will guide you through this situation.

The Reaction of Friends

Be prepared for adversity from your friends while you edit what your child is exposed to. Your friends may say you are being overprotective and unrealistic. So what? This is your child and the world will not protect him. So you must! You can modify your rules as your child matures and can understand the issues at hand. This can be difficult, but it is so important for your child.

Chapter 9

The Lord is near to all who call upon Him, to all who call upon Him in truth. (Psalm 145:18)

Answering Your Child's Questions About God And Other Religious Subjects

A child has lots of questions about the world around him. The more you expose him, the more the questions will come. If you take him to the zoo, he will ask about animals. If you go to a sporting event, questions will come up about the game. If you take him to church, he will ask about God. If you read him the Bible and teach him about Jesus, God and Mary, questions will be abundant in these subjects too. This is only natural as the child wants to know and understand everything! Be thankful he turns to you and asks rather than keeps it inside and wonders. It could be worse. He may ask his less knowledgeable little friends!

But how do you answer these often difficult, but very good questions? First of all, do not panic. Instead, say a silent, quick prayer like, "Dear God, please help me with this one!" Then be spontaneous, serious and attempt to be convincing. Remember your child thinks you are an expert and know everything. Therefore, you can often come up with an answer that makes sense and will please God! Try not to <u>over</u> answer a question. Keep your answer simple and brief. Your answer does not have to be profound. Satisfy his curiosity while teaching him religion. After answering the question, ask your child if he understands. "Does that sound like a good answer to you?" If he is confused or does not understand, repeat your answer, repeat with different words. Be patient, even if you must answer the question several times! If you seriously cannot come up with an answer, tell your child you do not know. "When we get home we'll look it up in the Bible" or "let's go by church and see if Father is there and maybe he can help us." Of course, these are less desirable because an hour later the issue will not be nearly as important to your child as it was when asked!

Following are examples of a few questions and some possible answers. There will be hundreds of questions. These samples are only to help you think about and prepare in advance for the type of questions which may come up as you teach your child your religion.

Q: **"Where is God? Why Can't We See Him?"**

A: "God lives in Heaven, way up above the sky. You know how daddy isn't with us right now. He is at work, and we can't see him. But we love him very much and think about him a lot. We know He loves us and thinks about us all the time. If we close our eyes we can pretend we see him, and He sees us the same way. That's a lot like how God is."

Q: **"How did God get to Heaven? Did He die, or what?"**

A: "God has always been in heaven. He was there before anything or anyone was ever made." (Introducing a little Baltimore Catechism!)

Q: **"When Can I See Jesus?"**

A: "Hopefully not for a long time. He lives in heaven with God. Some day you and I can both go visit Him. I think for now Jesus will let you stay with me. But we can talk to Him every day. When you pray and think about Jesus, He is near you."

Q: **"Why is Jesus' Heart Showing in that Picture?"** (of the Sacred Heart)

A "Jesus loves us very, very much. This is one way Jesus shows us how much He loves us. We love Him too!"

Q: **"Why is Father holding that cup and some bread up in the air?"**

A: "He is showing it to God and asking God to make it Holy and extra special. He is turning it into Jesus, just the way Jesus did at the Last Supper the night before He died on the cross."

Q: **"Why can't I have some bread and wine?"**

A: "When you get a little older you will learn more about God. Then you can have some."

Q: **"Why did those boys blow out those candles (pulpit) and light those over there (altar)?"**

A: "Over there (pulpit) they were reading the Bible and the candles showed that was special. Now the bread and wine is special and they are getting ready to bless them and turn them into Jesus here at this table."

Q: **"Can God be happy or sad?"**

A: Yes. God became man in Jesus Christ. He experienced and expressed human emotions. Jesus is God.

Q: **"How did Daniel get out of the hole that had the lions in it?"**

A: "I think some men put a ladder down there and helped him climb out."

Q: **"Why did Eve eat that apple even though God said not to?"**

A: "She thought it was OK not to mind God. She was wrong though, because God made her leave that beautiful garden since she didn't mind Him. It's really important to mind God and follow His rules like going to Church on Sunday, and not hurting people and loving God and loving your Mom and Dad."

The questions will be endless. They may be easy or difficult, but always a serious and important matter to your child. Do your best to answer it as such. Keep it simple!

Chapter 10

Stay sober and alert. Your opponent the devil is prowling like a roaring lion looking for someone to devour. Resist him, solid in your faith, realizing that the brotherhood of believers is undergoing the same sufferings throughout the world. (1 Peter 5:8-9)

Reject Temptation

Does your child have nightmares? Do you have nightmares? Are you tempted not to do certain things you know are good. Are there times you do not want to say night time prayers with your child because you are sleepy, or skip your morning prayer because it is a busy morning? Are there non-supportive people around you? Recognize these negative feelings and possibly difficult situations. They are temptations not to follow the Will of God, not to pray, not to teach your child your faith.

Teaching your child about God and His Mother will be very pleasing to God. Your relationship with the Holy Trinity and Our Lady will blossom and grow well beyond any of your expectations.

Remember, however, that anything pleasing to God will anger His opponent. Do not deny that the Devil really does exist! He is mentioned throughout the Bible. Be prepared to be tested and tempted. Jesus was tempted too, so do not be surprised if it happens to you!

Use Jesus as your example in handling the evil one. Like Jesus, when you feel temptation, when you sense the devil working on you, order him to leave; "Out of my home and my mind! In the Name of Our Lord Jesus Christ, get out of my heart and soul!" or "Get away from my spouse and my children. In the name of Jesus Christ, flee from our home!" If you use the name of Jesus, Satan is powerless.

If your child awakens with scary dreams, go to him and verbally bless him, crossing his forehead and praying to God to protect him. Hang a Rosary close to him. Sprinkle Holy Water around your home while asking God to bless each room. It will keep evil away!

Finally, you can invoke the help of you and your child's guardian angel who are always anxious to help "guard, rule and guide". Also, recite the prayer to St. Michael who is always helpful: The Prayer is:

"St. Michael the Archangel, defend us in the day of Battle; Be our protection against the wickedness and snares of the Devil. May God rebuke Him, we humbly pray, and do Thou, O prince of the Heavenly Host, by the power of God, cast into Hell, Satan and all the other evil spirits, who prowl through the world, seeking the ruin of souls. Amen"

By being alert, being prepared and asking the Holy Trinity for help, God and His goodness will prevail! <u>Do not</u>, do not, be afraid! Be strong, be determined! And flee to God who will always protect you!

Bibliography

Great books for children that you can find at your local Catholic bookstore.

The Bible Pictures for Little Eyes by Kenneth N. Taylor
My First Bible by Kenneth N. Taylor
The Beginners Bible by Joan Hutson
Dear God by Brimax Books
God Bless by Brimax Books
My Little Book of Prayers Illustrated by Kathy Allen
God Made Me by C.R. Gibson
A Little Book of Poems and Prayers by Joan Walsh Anglund
Poems and Prayers for the Very Young by Martha Alexander
Our Friends the Saints by W. H. Litho Company
The Saints by Louis M. Savary
Great Men of the Old Testament by Rev. Jude Winkler, O.F.M.
Great Women of the Old Testament by Rev. Jude Winkler, O.F.M.
Jesus Is Risen! by Palm Tree Press
Arch Book Bible Story Library (Excellent with simple rhyming and pictures)

Videos:
CCC of America:
The Day the Sun Danced: The True Story of Fatima
Bernadette: The Princess of Lourdes
Francis: The Knight of Assisi
Patrick: Brave Shepherd of the Emerald Isle
and many more!

Hanna-Barbera Productions:
The Nativity
Samson and Delilah
Daniel in the Lion's Den
Joshua and the Battle of Jericho
David and Goliath
Noah's Ark
Moses
The Easter Story
and many more!

Catholic Family Resouces

First contact your local Catholic Book & Gift Store for:
Bibles, books, vidoes, audios, scapulars, religious medals and gifts.

CCC of America: 1-800-929-0608

6000 Campus Circle Drive, Suite 110
Irving, TX 75063
Animated videos on Jesus and the Saints

Catholic Book Publishing:

The New Saint Joseph Baltimore Catechism
Picture Book of Saints
Available at your local Catholic store

Catholic City Internet Site: 1-216-333-9827

Box 614, Lakewood, OH 44107
http://www.catholicity.com
The *Internet Division* of the *Mary Foundation* offering
a broad range of FREE services including chat rooms, bulletin
boards and links to hundreds of Catholic/Family organizations. Also FREE Catholic novels and audio tapes.

R. B. Media: 217-546-5261

154 Doral, Springfield, IL 62704
Audio tapes on raising Roman Catholic children by
Stenson, Vitz, Isaacs and Von Hildebrand.

Holy Traders: 1-800-242-8467

1827 Stonehaven Drive, Boynton Beach, FL 33436
High quality trading cards featuring Catholic Saints.

Write for a FREE Catholic Resource Guide featuring
dozens of authentically Catholic Suppliers:

FREE Catholic Resource Guide
GOOD CATHOLIC BOOKS
Box 26144, Cleveland, OH 44126

How to Pray the Rosary

The Rosary was first given to Saint Dominic by our Blessed Mother. At Fatima, Lourdes and Guadalupe Our Lady asked Catholics to pray the rosary for repentance, the conversion of sinners and peace in the world.

FORM:

Sign of the Cross

The *Apostles Creed* on the crucifix

The *Our Father* on the large beads

The *Hail Mary* on the small beads

The *Glory Be to the Father* after the last *Hail Mary* of each decade

Fatima Prayer after each *Glory Be to the Father*:

> *O my Jesus, forgive us our sins, save us from the fires of hell, lead all souls to Heaven, especially those in most need of Thy mercy.*

Before reciting each decade, name a mystery of the Rosary (in sequence) and meditate on it during the decade.

THE JOYFUL MYSTERIES:

Pray on Mondays and Thursdays and all Sundays of Advent.

1. **The Annunciation-** Mary learns from the Angel Gabriel that God wishes her to become the Mother of God, and she humbly accepts. (*Luke 1:26-38*)

2. **The Visitation-** Mary goes to visit her cousin Elizabeth and is hailed as "Blessed". (*Luke 1:39-56*)

3. **The Nativity-** Mary gives birth to Jesus in a stable at Bethlehem. (*Luke 2:1-20*)

4. **The Presentation-** Mary and Joseph present Jesus to His Heavenly Father in the Temple (*Luke 2:22-39*)

5. **The Finding In The Temple-** After searching 3 days Mary and Joseph find Jesus teaching in the Temple. (*Luke 2:42-52*)

SORROWFUL MYSTERIES

Pray on Tuesdays and Fridays and all Sundays of Lent:

1. **Agony In The Garden-** The thought of our sins and His coming sufferings causes our agonizing Savior to sweat blood. (*Luke 22:41-45*)

2. **The Scourging-** Jesus' is stripped and unmercifully scourged until His body is one mass of bloody wounds. (*Matt. 27:26*)

3. **The Crowning With Thorns-** Jesus' claim to Kingship is ridiculed by a crown of thorns being placed on His head and a reed in His hand. (*Matt. 27:28-31*)

4. The Carrying Of The Cross- Jesus shoulders His cross and carries it to the place of crucifixion, while Mary follows Him sorrowfully.
(Luke 23:26-32)

5. The Crucifixion- Jesus dies, nailed to the cross, after 3 hours of agony witnessed by His Mother.
(Matthew 27:33-50)

GLORIOUS MYSTERIES

Pray on Wednesdays and Saturdays and all Sundays except Advent and Lent.

1. The Resurrection- Jesus rises from the dead on Easter Sunday, glorious and immortal.
(Matthew 28:5)

2. The Ascension- Jesus ascends into Heaven forty days after His Resurrection to sit at the right hand of God the Father from whence He shall return to judge the living and the dead.
(Luke 24:50-51)

3. The Descent Of The Holy Spirit- Jesus sends the Holy Spirit in the form of fiery tongues upon His Apostles and disciples.
(Acts 2:2-4)

4. The Assumption- Mary's soul returns to God and her body is assumed into Heaven and united with her soul.
(Revelations 12:1)

5. The Coronation- Mary is crowned as Queen of Heaven and Earth, Queen of Angels and Saints, that she may rule over all hearts in time and in eternity.
(Judith 15:10-11)

HAIL HOLY QUEEN

Hail, Holy Queen, Mother of mercy; our life, our sweetness, our hope. To thee do we cry, poor banished children of Eve. To thee do we send up our sighs, mourning and weeping in this valley of tears. Turn then, most gracious Advocate thine eyes of mercy towards us and, after this our exile, show us the blessed fruit of Thy womb, Jesus. O clement, O loving, O sweet Virgin Mary.
R. Pray for us, O holy Mother of God.
V. That we may be worthy of the promises of Christ.

LET US PRAY

O God whose only begotten Son by his life, death and Resurrection has purchased for us the rewards of eternal life; grant we beseech thee, that meditating on these mysteries of the Most Holy Rosary of the Blessed Virgin Mary, we may imitate what they contain and obtain what they promise through the same Christ our Lord. Amen.

THE APOSTLES' CREED

I believe in God, the Father Almighty, Creator of heave and earth; and in Jesus Christ his only son, Our Lord; who was conceived by the Holy Spirit, born of the Virgin Mary, suffered under Pontius Pilate, was crucified, died, and was buried. He descended into Hell; the third day He arose again form the dead; He ascended into heaven, sits at he right hand of God the Father Almighty; from whence He shall come to judge the living and the dead I believe in the Holy Spirit, the holy Catholic Church, the communion of saints, the forgiveness of sins, the resurrection of the body, and life everlasting. Amen

OUR FATHER

*O*ur Father, Who art in heaven, hallowed be thy name. Thy kingdom; thy will be done on earth, as it is in heaven. Give us this day our daily bread; and forgive us our trepasses, as we forgive those who trespass against us. And lead us not into temptation, but deliver us from evil. Amen

HAIL MARY

*H*ail Mary, full of grace; the Lord is with thee; blessed art thou among women, and blessed is the fruit of thy womb, Jesus. Holy Mary, Mother of God, pray for us sinners, now and at the hour of our death. Amen.

GLORY BE TO THE FATHER

*G*lory be the Father, and to the Son, and the Holy Spirit. As it was in the beginning, is now, and ever shall be, world without end. Amen.

FRUITS OF THE MYSTERIES OF THE ROSARY:

JOYFUL

Annunciation	Humility
Visitation	Fraternal Charity
Nativity	Spiritual Values
Presentation	Purity and Obedience
Finding in the Temple	Fidelity to one's duties

SORROWFUL

Agony in the Garden	Sorrow for Sin
Scourging at the Pillar	Mortification of the Senses
Crowning with Thorns	Love of Humiliation
Carrying of the Cross	Bearing of Trials
Crucifixion	Forgiveness of Injuries

GLORIOUS

Resurrection	Faith and Hope
Ascension	Desire of Heaven
Descent of the Holy Spirit	The Gifts of the Holy Spirit
Assumption	Devotion to Mary
Coronation	Perseverance

Favorite Roman Catholic Prayers

GUARDIAN ANGEL:

Angel of God my guardian dear to whom God's love commits me here. Ever this day be at my side to light, to guard, to rule and guide. Amen.

ANGELUS (noon daily):

The angel of the Lord declared unto Mary.

R. And she conceived of the Holy Spirit.
Hail Mary, etc.

V. Behold the handmaid of the Lord.

R. Be it done unto me according to Thy word.
Hail Mary, etc.

V. AND THE WORD WAS MADE FLESH.

R. And dwelt among us.
Hail Mary, etc.

V. Pray for us O Holy Mother of God.

R. That we may be worthy of the promises of Christ.
LET US PRAY: Pour forth, we beseech Thee, O Lord, Thy grace into our hearts; that we to whom the Incarnation of Christ, Thy Son was made known by a message of an angel, may by His Passion and Cross, be brought to the glory of His Resurrection through the same Christ our Lord. Amen.

SAINT MICHAEL THE ARCHANGEL:

Saint Michael the Archangel, defend us in battle. Be our protection against the wickedness and snares of the devil; May God rebuke him we humbly pray; And do thou O Prince of the heavenly hosts, by the power of God, thrust in hell Satan and all evils spirit, who wander the world for the ruin of souls. Amen

MEMORARE OF ST. BERNARD:

Remember, O most gracious Virgin Mary, that never was it known that any one who fled to thy protection, implored thy help, and sought thy intercession, was left unaided. Inspired with this confidence, I fly unto Thee, O Virgin of virgins, my Mother, to thee I come, before thee I stand sinful and sorrowful. O Mother of the Word Incarnate! despise not my petitions, but in thy mercy, hear, and answer me. Amen.

SAINT THERESE, THE LITTLE FLOWER:

Please pick me a Rose from the heavenly garden and send it to me with a message of love. Ask God to grant me the favor I thee implore and tell him I will love him each day more and more.

Parent's Favorite Catholic Prayers

SAINT ANN'S PRAYER (MOTHER'S PRAYER)

Saint Ann, my dear mother and most compassionate protectress, receive graciously my poor efforts to do you honor. May I ever be devoted to you with a heart full of child-like humility and submission. May your example encourage me, your intercession strengthen me, your goodness consore me! Permit me with all my heart to commend you to my children. As you consecrated Mary, your child of Grace, entirely to God. I beg you to obtain for me to the grace to train my children for Him, and with them to labor perseveringly for heaven. As you lived in holy harmony with Saint Joachim, so may love, union, devotion, and the zeal for virtue reign my household, that we may belong to that host of blessed spouses who with you will love, praise, and glorify the Most High forever and ever. Amen.

PRAYER TO SAINT JOSEPH (FATHER'S PRAYER)

O Saint Joseph, whose protection is so great, so strong, so prompt before the throne of God, I place in thee all my interests and desires. Do thou O Saint Joseph, assist me by thy powerful intercession and obtain for me from thy divine Son all spiritual blessings, through Jesus Christ, Our Lord, so that having engaged here below thy heavenly power, I may offer my thanksgiving and homage to the most loving of fathers. O Saint Joseph, I never weary contemplating thee and Jesus asleep thy arms; I dare not approach while He reposes near thy heart. Press Him in my name and kiss His fine head for me, and ask Him to return the kiss when I draw my dying breath. Saint Joseph, Patron of departing souls, pray for me. Amen.

Children's Favorite Catholic Prayers

ACT OF CONTRITION

Oh, my God, I am sorry for my sins with all my heart. In choosing to do wrong, and failing to do good. I have sinned against you whom I should love above all things. I firmly intend, with the help of Your Grace, To confess my sins, to do penance, to sin no more and to avoid the near occasion of sin. Our Savior Jesus Christ suffered and died for us. In His name, my God, have mercy. Amen.

YOUNG CHILDREN'S THANKSGIVING PRAYER

Thank you God for he world so sweet.
Thank you God for the food we eat.
Thank you God for the birds that sing.
Thank you for everything! Amen.

PRAYER TO THE SACRED HEART OF JESUS

Most Sacred Heart of Jesus, have Mercy on us.
Sweet Heart of Jesus, I put my trust in you.

PRAYER TO THE IMMACULATE HEART OF MARY

Most Pure Heart of Mary, keep my heart free from sin.
Sweet Heart of Mary, be my salvation.

SIMPLE CHILDREN'S PRAYER BEFORE COMMUNION

My Jesus, I need You. It's hard for me to be good.
Come to make my soul strong. Give my soul it's Food and Drink
Let me grow in Love for You. Amen

SIMPLE CHILDREN'S PRAYER AFTER COMMUNION

My Jesus I love you. Thank you for coming to me.
Stay with me always. I need Your help to be good.
Help me to be more like you. Amen.

Parent's Favorite Catholic Saints

SAINT JOSEPH *(March 19)*
Husband of Mary, Patron of the Universal Church
A lowly carpenter of the House of David he was the pure spouse of the Blessed Virgin Mary. A "just man" chosen by God to be the protector of Jesus. He is a father's model for charity, chastity and fortitude.

SAINT ANTHONY OF PADUA *(June 13)*
Priest, Doctor of the Church, Patron of the Poor and Lost Articles.
A Franciscan missionary, who converted thousands as a preacher and "wonderworker". His tongue is still incorrupt (not deteriorated). His relics are cherished and his reputation for miracles is worldwide.

SAINT ANNE *(July 26)*
The Patroness of Mothers and Housewives
Her name means "grace". She was the mother of the Blessed Virgin Mary and grandmother of Jesus. Along with her husband Joachim had been without children until angel said they will have a daughter, who will be honored by all the world. She is a mothers model of love and faith.

SAINT JOACHIM *(July 26)*
Father of the Blessed Virgin Mary, Patron of Fathers
Of the Tribe of Judah and the House of David, he lived in Nazareth. He fasted and prayed for 40 days in the desert to have children. An angel appeared to him saying his prayers would be answered.

SAINT MAXIMILLION KOLBE *(August 14)*
Priest, Martyr, Founder of the Knights of the Immaculate
A Franciscan, ill most of his life, he was devoted to the Blessed Virgin and used modern technology to reach millions. He died a Martyr in Auschwitz, the Nazi death camp.

SAINT MONICA *(August 27)*
Patroness of Mothers
She was the mother of Saint Augustine. After great trials along with patience she prayed fervently for the conversion of her son. Mothers have implored her help in times of trial.

SAINT THERESE OF THE CHILD JESUS-THE LITTLE FLOWER *(October 1)*
Virgin, Patron of Missions
She was cured by the Blessed Virgin as a child. As a Carmelite nun she offered all her little sacrifices to help priests save souls. She is a highly favored Saint and is always pictured with beautiful roses.

SAINT JUDE *(October 28)*
Apostles, Martyr, Patron of Impossible Cases.
The cousin of Jesus, he was a missionary with Saint Simon in Persia where they preached and healed, making many converts. His Relics are honored in Saint Peter's Basilica in Rome.

Children's Favorite Catholic Saints

SAINT SEBASTIAN *(January 20)*
Martyr, Patron of Athletes
The son of wealthy parents he became the captain of the Roman Guard protecting the Emperor. He was accused of following Jesus and was persecuted. Before the Emperor had him killed he healed and tended to the needs of many prisoners.

SAINT AGNES *(January 21)*
Virgin, Martyr, Patroness of Children of Mary
As a beautiful young girl she refused to be married choosing Jesus as her spouse. She was persecuted, yet she still praised Jesus. She died making the sign of the cross. This gentle saint's name means lamb.

SAINT DOMINIC SAVIO *(March 9)*
Patron of Children
An Italian boy who at age 5 became an altar boy. He told Saint John Bosco he wanted to be a priest. He studied hard and loved to pray. His schoolmates liked his kindness and cheerfulness. But he was ill and died saying "What beautiful things I see!"

SAINT JOAN OF ARC *(May 30)*
Virgin, Martyr, Patroness of Soldiers
A young pheasant girl with pious parents she had a special devotion to Saint Michael the Archangel. She lead a small army under the banner of Jesus and Mary to conquer her country's enemies.

SAINT ALOYSUIS GONZAGA *(June 21)*
Religious, Patron of Youth
A young prince who gave up all to follow Jesus. He became a novice and nursed the victims of an epidemic in Rome. Before reaching the priesthood he died from illness while gazing at a crucifix.

SAINT MARIA GORETTI *(July 6)*
Virgin, Martyr, Patroness of Youth
An obedient and happy Italian farm girl who was attacked by an evil boy. She resisted his evil, then forgave him and prayed for his repentance before she died. After prison the evil boy sought forgiveness and became a Capuchin laybrother.

SAINT CLARE *(August 11)*
Virgin, Patroness of Sore Eyes and Television, Foundress of the Poor Clares.
As a young girl from a noble family, she gave herself to Jesus and a life of poverty, prayer and fasting. She worked with Saint Francis and was devoted to the Blessed Sacrament.

SAINT FRANCIS OF ASSISI *(October 4)*
Patron of Catholic Action, Founder of the Franciscans
He left his wealthy family to devote his life to Jesus in poverty as a missionary preaching repentence, faith and peace with all men. He was a stigmatist bearing the five wounds of Christ. He's also known as the protector of animals.

WRITE US!

1) <u>FREE Catholic Resource Guide</u>
   Includes over a 50 Roman Catholic organizations
   with pratical products, services and information for families.

2) <u>GUIDING YOUR CATHOLIC PRESCHOOLER</u>
   Feedback
   What did you think? Good or Bad?
   What could we do better?

3) <u>Authors, Artists and Creative Types</u>
   Contact us with your creative ideas and suggestions
   to help families raise their children Roman Catholic.
   (*Manuscripts welcome, include SASE*)

Write to:

GOOD CATHOLIC BOOKS Box 26144, Cleveland, OH 44126

About GOOD CATHOLIC BOOKS:
It was started to provide quality products for Catholic families
at affordable prices. Our mission is to help families bring up
their children in the Roman Catholic Faith.

How can you help?

1) Pray for us.
2) Keep in touch, let us know what you think
   and how we can improve.
3) Pray the Rosary daily for the Pope, the Holy
   Roman Catholic Church, Catholic families,
   your local parish and Pastor.

Finally, tell your friends and family about us.

Thanks and God Bless!

IF YOU REALLY LIKE THIS BOOK...

Consider Giving it Away

Parents
Grandparents
Parishes/Pastors
Preschool Teachers
Librarians
Religious Education Directors

Complete the order form on the other side of this page and send to:

Good Catholic Books
Box 26144
Cleveland, OH 44126

If this is your last page, please photocopy the order form and freely distribute to your friends.

Guiding Your
Catholic Preschooler

Help Others Enjoy It!

Parents – give copies to your friends as a gift.

Grandparents – give it as a gift to your kids and relatives.

Parishes/Pastors – give it to your parishioners as a Baptism gift.

Teachers – use it as a Resource Guide, recommend it to parents.

Librarians – make it part of your Parenting/Family section.

Contact your Family, Friends, Pastor, Neighbors, Religious Education Director, Preschool Teachers and Librarians.

Ideal for Baptisms, Easter, Christmas, Anniversaries and Birthdays!

Call your local Catholic Book & Gift Store or write:

GOOD CATHOLIC BOOKS
Box 26144, Cleveland, OH 44126

IF YOU REALLY LIKE THIS BOOK...

Consider Giving it Away

Parents
Grandparents
Parishes/Pastors
Preschool Teachers
Librarians
Religious Education Directors

Complete the order form on the other side of this page and send to:

Good Catholic Books
Box 26144
Cleveland, OH 44126

If this is your last page, please photocopy the order form and freely distribute to your friends.

Guiding Your
Catholic Preschooler

Help Others Enjoy It!

Parents – give copies to your friends as a gift.

Grandparents – give it as a gift to your kids and relatives.

Parishes/Pastors – give it to your parishioners as a Baptism gift.

Teachers – use it as a Resource Guide, recommend it to parents.

Librarians – make it part of your Parenting/Family section.

*Contact your Family, Friends, Pastor, Neighbors, Religious
Education Director, Preschool Teachers and Librarians.*

Ideal for Baptisms, Easter, Christmas,
Anniversaries and Birthdays!

Call your local Catholic Book & Gift Store or write:

GOOD CATHOLIC BOOKS
Box 26144, Cleveland, OH 44126

Please send me _____ copies of **GUIDING YOUR CATHOLIC
PRESCHOOLER** (US$2.99 each). I am enclosing $_____
*(please add US $1.00 to cover shipping. Ohio residents please add
appropriate sales tax).* Send check or money order – no cash or C.O.D.'s
...ase. Allow up to 2 weeks for delivery.
(Call about quantity discounts 216-356-6139)

Name _____

Parish _____

Address _____

City_____ State_____ Zip _____

Phone number (   )_____ # Kids _____

How did you get your copy? _____

_____

Comments: _____

_____

❑ *Send me the* **FREE** *Catholic Resource Guide, check here!*

IF YOU REALLY LIKE THIS BOOK...

Consider Giving it Away

Parents
Grandparents
Parishes/Pastors
Preschool Teachers
Librarians
Religious Education Directors

Complete the order form on the other side of this page and send to:

Good Catholic Books
Box 26144
Cleveland, OH 44126

If this is your last page, please photocopy the order form and freely distribute to your friends.

Guiding Your
Catholic Preschooler

Help Others Enjoy It!

Parents – give copies to your friends as a gift.

Grandparents – give it as a gift to your kids and relatives.

Parishes/Pastors – give it to your parishioners as a Baptism gift.

Teachers – use it as a Resource Guide, recommend it to parents.

Librarians – make it part of your Parenting/Family section.

Contact your Family, Friends, Pastor, Neighbors, Religious Education Director, Preschool Teachers and Librarians.

Ideal for Baptisms, Easter, Christmas, Anniversaries and Birthdays!

Call your local Catholic Book & Gift Store or write:

GOOD CATHOLIC BOOKS
Box 26144, Cleveland, OH 44126

Please send me _____ copies of **GUIDING YOUR CATHOLIC PRESCHOOLER** (US$2.99 each). I am enclosing $_____ *(please add US $1.00 to cover shipping. Ohio residents please add appropriate sales tax).* Send check or money order – no cash or C.O.D.'s please. Allow up to 2 weeks for delivery.
(Call about quantity discounts 216-356-6139)

Name _____

Parish _____

Address _____

City_____ State_____ Zip _____

Phone number (___)_____ # Kids _____

How did you get your copy? _____

_____

Comments: _____

_____

❑ *Send me the* **FREE** *Catholic Resource Guide, check here!*